D1535421

Twits in Love

A STEAMPUNK DISTRACTION

TOM ALAN ROBBINS

BOOK ONE OF THE TWITS CHRONICLES

What People Are Saying:

"The Twits Chronicles are hilarious, blessed with truly exceptional dialogue. Steampunk dystopia meets Oscar Wildean wit in these books. I found myself laughing out loud on numerous occasions--and that's not something I often do while reading. "
—Nick Sullivan, author of The Deep Series and Zombie Bigfoot.

"Delightful! A frothy frappe of P.G. Wodehouse and steam-punk. If you're the sort who reads blurbs before reading the book, stop it. Stop it right now. Read TWITS IN LOVE and have a good time. These days we can all use a bit more of a good time."

—John Ostrander, American writer of comic books, including *Suicide Squad*, *Grimjack* and *Star Wars: Legacy*.

"I haven't enjoyed the company of such eccentric characters since A Confederacy of Dunces, and Tom Alan Robbins has managed to place them in the stylized world of Oscar Wilde. A really unique journey."
— Kevin Conroy, Actor, The voice behind the DC Comics superhero Batman .

"Tom Alan Robbins' Twits stories are hilarious, thought provoking and mind bending. His juicy turns of phrase will stick in your ear like a catchy song."
— Michael Urie, Actor, Producer and Director

"Tom is the most talented, delicious writer. Do yourself a favor, and immerse yourself in the fabulous world of TWITS!"
— Mary Testa, 3 time Tony Award Nominee

The Author makes no representation of any kind as to his being a citizen of the United Kingdom, either native or naturalized. He is from a small town in Ohio, for which he apologizes.

Cover design by Melody J. Barber of Aurora Publicity

Additional designs by Eric Wright of The Puppet Kitchen.

Twits Logo designed by Feppa Rodriquez

Proofreading by Gretchen Tannert Douglas

For Spike, who made my life and Rose who made it mean something.

Foreword

The origins of the Twits Chronicles can be traced back to November of 2016, when my friend Nick Sullivan (author of "The Deep Series" of Caribbean mystery novels) asked me to participate in a round-robin writing project. He had assembled a group of talented authors who were each going to write the first chapter of a book, which the other authors would take turns adding chapters to until it was finished. My contribution was based on an idea that I had been kicking around for some years. This is the scenario I laid out for the group to follow:

> "Scientific progress has eliminated every obstacle to human happiness. There is no more hunger, poverty, disease or war. The problem is—now what? What do we do with our time between birth and death? The answer seems to be that we try to amuse ourselves. This sort of

thing has happened throughout history. Classes have sprung up whose wealth and privilege has set them above the need to strive. The upper class in Victorian England is an example… the robber barons of the time of Gatsby, the French nobles pre-revolution. The result seems to be that an elaborate ritualistic society emerges in which people strive for status and live for pleasure. In the world I'm imagining, everybody is in the same boat and the game is all there is.,

I've begun with a take on the Bertie Wooster/Jeeves books combined with a steampunk world in which electricity never got discovered and everything runs on hydrogen and steam.

Cyril Chippington-Smythe lives in sybaritic splendor with his loyal servant, a steam-powered robot named Bentley (produced by a company descended from the one that built the classic luxury automobiles). He has no ambition other than pleasure. He is endlessly optimistic. He means well but has trouble asserting himself. He drinks too much.

Bentley is superhuman. He is loyal, brilliant and discreet. He anticipates Cyril's every need. He is the closest thing Cyril has to a parent.

Cheswick Wickford-Davies is Cyril's cousin, and the closest thing to a friend he has. He is weak, cowardly and lacks any moral fiber. His one passion is Alice Witherspoon. He would do anything to possess her.

Alice Witherspoon is an aggressive, toothy aristocrat. She takes her superiority for granted. She has decided to marry Cyril whether he likes it or not. She is always in the right (in her own mind)."

Based on this scenario, I wrote my first chapter and passed it along to the group, which came up with a series of incredible and imaginative adventures involving time travel, alternate dimensions and subversive revolutionary groups before I brought it to a close with the attempted destruction of the world's hydrogen plants. I thought at that point that I was done with these characters, but Nick kept poking at me to go back to my first chapter and do my own take on the story. I persisted in batting his hand away and whining at him to leave me alone.

Then came the pandemic. I sat in my apartment like everyone else—terrified of public spaces and fellow humans. "Aha!" thought I, "the perfect time to get some writing done..." but nothing would come. Whatever I started seemed trivial compared to the earth-shaking events taking place outside. Finally, I looked at my old chapter of Twits in Love. Perhaps, instead of trying to write something meaningful that would only be trivialized by reality, I should try to write something trivial to escape what was all-too-real.

And, Dear Reader, that is why you hold this book in your hands (or on your screen). Strangely enough, in trying to write something trivial, I found more meaning in the material than I intended. I discovered that my aristocrats and their construct of a society were much more interesting if they were surrounded by a dystopian world of climate change and species extinction. I intend to keep writing about these characters as long as there are readers who enjoy their exploits. More stories are on the way.

Death Before Dishonour!

Tom Alan Robbins

Steampunk

"Steampunk is a subgenre of science fiction that incorporates retrofuturistic technology and aesthetics inspired by 19th-century industrial steam-powered machinery. Steampunk works are often set in an alternative history of the Victorian era or the American "Wild West", where steam power remains in mainstream use, or in a fantasy world that similarly employs steam power."

Wikipedia

A Word About Timelines

For those who are unfamiliar with the Steampunk genre, a word about timelines may be helpful. The Steampunk Universe in which The Twits Chronicles take place is clearly not our own. That is why events and cultural references that happened in vastly different eras in our own world seem to happen in a compressed time period. It feels as if we are in a vaguely Victorian era, and yet there are references to events and quotations from well into the twentieth century.

It may help to think of this as an exercise in "what if?" What if electricity wasn't discovered until much later in human history? Human ingenuity would still search for new ways of using existing technology, and so steam power and mechanical engineering would keep advancing, while much of the aesthetic of the world around us could remain in the nineteenth century.

The world that would result is the world of *The Twits Chronicles*. Other writers would use these same criteria to create very different realities. This is mine.

Enter and enjoy.

Contents

CHAPTER ONE

I Am Awakened

Alcohol is like the cousin who owes you money. It promises everything and delivers nothing. I had hearkened to its siren song the previous evening and now I floated dreamlessly in a sea of regret. Waking could bring only pain and I clung to the darkness as a writer clings to a simile. Alas, I was finally ripped from slumber by my valet, who cleared his throat like a tenor getting a running start at a high C. I tentatively waggled a toe and upon this sign of consciousness he whipped open the bedroom curtains and unleashed the sun's cruel rays upon my helpless carcass. Sunlight is a beastly thing after a night of carousing and I can see why vampires in novels are always complaining about it.

My eyes rolled wildly in their sockets, which seemed to be filled with sand. "For the love of God, Bentley, why this cruel letting in of light? Why this throat clearing and foot tapping?"

For those of you who have not had the good fortune to meet Bentley, he is a sleek-headed, heavy-lidded gent with a ramrod posture and a perfect triangle of a nose. He is also a steam-powered automaton with a degree of moral certainty that only a machine could possess.

"It is nine o'clock, Sir. Miss Witherspoon is joining you for breakfast in thirty minutes."

The mention of Alice Witherspoon jolted me upright as though Bentley had poked me in the kidneys with a cattle prod. If, as Bernard Shaw once said, "There are those that look at things the way they are, and ask why?", Alice was the sort of specimen who looked at things the way they are and snapped, "Stop it at once!"

I struggled weakly to escape my bedclothes. "Joining me for breakfast? Has the earth tilted on its axis? Has Armageddon come in on little cat feet? Why is this horrible thing happening?"

"You invited her, Sir, last night."

An icy hand gripped my vitals. I grasped the bedpost to stop the room from spinning. "I didn't say anything compromising, did I, Bentley? I made no promises? She's made no secret of her intention to slap on the fetters and deliver me to the altar like a spoil of war."

"I was able to drip hot soup on Sir's neck at one particularly maudlin moment, but I could not say what transpired while I was brûléeing the crèmes."

"You shouldn't have left me alone with her for a moment! You know how malleable I am when I'm in my cups."

"You can assume a putty-like quality, if I may say so, Sir."

"This is awful! For all we know I could be engaged to that fanged medusa as we speak!"

Bentley began bustling about the room. "We must endeavor to ascertain your position at breakfast."

"Alcohol is a dreadful thing." I eyed him speculatively. "Have you got any?"

"I took the liberty of preparing an eye-opener."

I don't know where Bentley got the recipe for his morning-after libation. Some say he met Lucifer at a crossroads and traded his immortal soul for it. This, of course, is impossible as he has no soul. Bentley held out a goblet on a silver tray and I gratefully tossed it down the old gulper.

"Ambrosia! I'm going to need a second coat if I'm to eat opposite Miss Witherspoon. Those enormous teeth gnashing and grinding rather put one off one's chow." I rubbed my head vigorously. "It's so unnecessary! The art of false teeth has entered its golden age. They're making them out of ground-up seashells and glue or some such, I hear."

"Perhaps you should mention it to her at breakfast."

"And have her sink that jagged portcullis into my neck? No, thank you." I shook my head mournfully. "Ah, Bentley, life is a vale of... something or other."

"Tears, Sir?"

"Oh, I don't think so. Is it?"

"So the poets would have us believe."

"Well... poets—we know what they are—always smelling the daisies and trying to borrow a ten-spot until some gazette comes through with a check."

"There's just time for the morning cannon, Sir."

I smoothed the shining sheet of hair that clung to my scalp and sighed. "Right ho. Open the window, there's a good chap."

He slid open the sash with a squeal and rolled the family cannon up to the opening. It was a shiny old brass thing whose origins were lost to antiquity.

"I think a half charge today, Bentley. The old noggin is rather tender."

"Very good, Sir."

He poured in the powder and rammed home the wadding. Handing me the lanyard he gazed inward at some mysterious time-keeping apparatus.

"Three, two, one..."

"Death before dishonour," I cried, yanking at the cord. There was a satisfying "boom!" which was answered by my neighbors' artillery up and down the street. Cries of "Death before dishonour!" echoed from the cobblestones.

"Thank you, Bentley. Quite satisfactory."

He wheeled the smoking heirloom back into the corner and began laying out my morning ensemble. As he leaned over to place an extremely tasteful tie next to a crisply ironed shirt, I caught the scent of hot oil.

"I say, are you running a little warm today?"

"Nothing serious, Sir. A clogged pressure release valve. I shall attend to it."

"Please do. I can't have you in the shop with Alice swooping about." I shuddered. "Righto. Flick on the shower, would you?"

Bentley slid into the bathroom like a pat of butter on a hot pan and I heard the pitter-patter of water I knew would be calibrated to the perfect temperature. I felt almost... happy. He leaned his upper torso back into the bedroom.

"This might be an apropos moment to mention that Mr. Wickford-Davies has been waiting on the stairs since eight o'clock."

The burgeoning happiness within me lost the will to live and moped off to smoke a cigarette.

"Binky? What on earth does he want?"

"He did not take me into his confidence."

"Why have you left him so callously on the stairs?"

"He claims to prefer the stairs. He states that stairs only force you to choose up or down, whereas life is a miasma of impossible decisions that all lead to the grave."

I furrowed my brow. "Give me a minute to get into the shower, pump one of your pick-me-uppers down his throat and lead him in."

"Yes, Sir."

"You might offer him a sandwich."

"There are no sandwiches."

I gaped at him in astonishment! "How can that be? Civilization is founded upon the belief that sandwiches will always be readily available."

"I'm afraid we're on rather short rations at the moment. The food production facility at Weasel-on-Stoat was bombed."

"Who would do such a thing?"

"The act was attributed to anarchists."

"Oh." I considered for a moment. "I have nothing against anarchy so long as it doesn't disrupt the minutiae of daily life, but if it destroys the social contract between us and our sandwiches I'm afraid I must turn a cold shoulder."

"I shall fetch Mr. Wickford-Davies, Sir."

If alcohol is one's down-at-heels cousin, Binky is one's actual cousin and is likewise a deadbeat. Cheswick Wickford-Davies (Binky to his friends, if he had any) has elevated sponging to an art form. He is related to practically everyone and is so skilled at inviting himself to one thing and another that I don't believe he sees his home for weeks at a time. He survives by gnawing on the ankle of some distant uncle who grudgingly sends a small allowance each month. Binky is reliably good company, or was until he fell like a hod of bricks for Alice Witherspoon's buck-toothed charms. I have a particularly vigorous shower, but even through the cataract I could hear his sighs. They gradually gained in volume until I gave up and turned off the taps.

"What ho, old sot. Why all this puffing like a grampus and so on?"

He gazed at me like a terrier who has lost his faith in balls. "I've come to say goodbye, Cyril."

"Surely not. You just got here. Hand me my robe."

He hefted the flimsy bit of silk as though the pockets were stuffed with lead and managed to toss it weakly at my ankles. "Death before dishonour," he whispered hoarsely.

"Death before dishonour." I examined him closely. "This is a dismal sight."

"You shan't have to bear it long. I'm leaving for Antarctica on the next dirigible."

"What on earth are you going to do in Antarctica?"

"I'll find something. I'm sure I can pick up a few coppers sweeping the ice or some such."

"No ice in Antarctica, *mon frère*. That's an Old Wives Tale."

"Or shooing the penguins away."

"Are there still penguins? Perhaps you should make sure before you run off to herd them."

He kicked weakly at a fallen pillow. "Damn the Great Extinction!"

"Slow down, old cock. I haven't had my coffee yet. You say you are going to Antarctica to herd possibly illusory sea fowl but you don't get at the root of the mystery. Why are you fleeing your home and family?"

"I have to stop my mind from dwelling on her, Cyril. Backbreaking physical labor in a harsh climate will leave no time for pining."

"I don't know how backbreaking it would be to shoo penguins. They had a reputation for being more or less docile."

He glared at me balefully. "How could you understand—you, who are the object of her adoration?"

I began to catch up. "You mean Alice?"

"The syllables of her name pierce me like the fangs of adders."

"Crooked, over-sized fangs, I'm sure."

"Don't joke. Just shake my hand and wish me well."

"I do wish you well. My fondest hope is that she leaps out of my life and into your arms. I don't know why she resists you. Your taste in clothing is impeccable and most of the other virtues begin with dressing well."

He sighed. "Thank you, old chum." His eyes took on a shifty flavour.

"Um... look here, do you suppose you could lend me the money for the airship? I'm a little short at the moment."

"Of course. I'm sure you'll pay it back in no time from your wages in the penguin herding industry."

Bentley wafted into the room bearing coffee. The smell of burning oil accompanied him.

"Ahoy, Bentley, you're overheating to an odoriferous degree."

"I beg your pardon, Sir. I shall attend to it between the fruity slices and the omelet."

My vitals cried out for sustenance. A muffled bleat like a lost lamb emanated from my midsection. "Jolly good. Cheesy omelet, is it?"

"Yes, Sir."

"Real eggs?"

"Nearly, Sir."

"Oh, well."

"Miss Witherspoon has arrived. I have placed her in the morning room."

Binky whirled around like a vole who hears the hoot of a barn owl. "Do you mean to say she's here?"

"Now don't go to pieces, old crumb. We're having breakfast."

He goggled at me accusingly. "How could you?"

"I assure you I would never have invited her in my right mind. Apparently, I was suffering from acute alcohol poisoning. That's not the worst of it. In my drunken stupor there is a distinct possibility that I may have put my neck into the noose."

The color drained from his face. "You haven't proposed! That would be the end of me."

"I don't know! That's the point. That's what I hope to discover at breakfast."

"I come to you for solace and find a knife lodged between my shoulder blades."

"Look, old sausage, if by some horrible chance I have allowed myself to be ensnared by that harridan I shall move heaven and earth to escape. I will flee to the far corners of the globe. She shall not have me. This I swear! Now, come and say hello."

"I can't see her."

"Be a man! You can't go ducking into doorways and running off to Antarctica every time Alice sets her paddle-like foot onto the fairway."

He slumped like a frozen custard in a heat wave. "What else can I do?"

Suddenly a light went on in what some laughingly refer to as my brain. "Here, let's ask Bentley!"

"By Jove, that's brilliant! No one can top Bentley in the thinking department. What about it?"

Bentley's expression didn't change, but the odor of stale petroleum grew sharper. There was a sound of gears turning. "With all due modesty, Sir, my particular model is known for its powers of analytical thinking."

"Cogitate on this: I want to be rid of Alice; Binky wants to possess her, body and soul. Can the transfer of her affections be achieved?"

A distinct whirring sound emanated from deep within Bentley's stately cranium. Only a tiny flicker of his optical sensors betrayed the mammoth computational task taking place behind his serene expression. Binky stared at him worshipfully.

"It's epic, isn't it? Like the Oracle at Delphi."

A tiny puff of steam drifted from Bentley's left ear and he returned to the mortal plane.

"Well? Have you cracked it?"

"I believe so, Sir. It is generally accepted that in matters of romance, people want most acutely what they cannot have. The popular literature is rife with examples."

"But she *can* have him. His desperation to fling his corporeal and spiritual selves at her is manifest."

"It will require subterfuge."

Binky brightened at once. "By Jove, I've always been drawn to the stage. Cyril, you remember what a keen thespian I was in school. I was rather good in that Oscar Wilde thing if you recall."

I did and he wasn't. "You know that you spit when you declaim."

"I don't."

"I suppose it could be condensation or some sort of spontaneous liquefaction of your leading ladies."

"I don't spit!"

"Fine. Have it your way. What's the story line, Bentley?"

"The usual ploy is to invent an alternative love interest. This brings the desired object's jealousy into play. Combining this with an icy reserve toward Miss Witherspoon should bring the desired result."

Binky positively gleamed. "Genius! You're wasted in service, Bentley. You should run for public office."

"Heaven forfend! Even a simulacrum has its pride."

"Let's try it out at once! Come on, Cyril. I'll join you and Alice for breakfast."

I eyed him coolly. "I don't recall inviting you."

"Thanks awfully. I'd love to."

"Bentley, can you whip up another cheesy omelet?"

"I shall simply make them smaller, Sir."

The lamb within me cried out again. "That seems rather hard on me. I love cheesy omelets."

Binky snorted. "This is not the time to cavil about cheesy omelets! Love is a higher imperative."

I could see that any attempt to impede him would end in violence. "Lead on."

Binky didn't hear me, as he was already halfway down the stairs. I hastened to catch up and stopped him at the entrance to the morning room.

"Let me go in first, old chum, then you saunter in as if you hadn't a care in the world."

"Don't worry, I have a plan."

"Please don't say that. It sends shivers down my spine."

He gripped my arms and looked into my eyes with a kind of eager ferocity.

"I'm depending on you!"

I stared back at him. "Honestly, we've known each other all our lives. How can you put your faith in such a leaky vessel?"

"Bentley knows what he's doing. Just stick to the plan."

"Look, old stain, I shall do my utmost, especially as the success of your venture will save me from the clutches of that harpy. Now turn me loose."

I disentangled myself from his grasp and flung open the door to the morning room, where I found Alice and her teeth leafing angrily through a pile of recent periodicals. I had known Alice since we wrestled one another to a draw at dancing school. She had a terrifying certainty about virtually everything, and had determined early on that she and I were destined for each other. I have sometimes wondered what I might have accomplished with all of the energy I have expended in fighting her off over the years. For example, I had always dreamed of inventing a new knot for neckties that would be named after me. Lost opportunities. Sad.

"Good morning, Cyril. Death before dishonour."

"Death before dishonour."

She turned a page and snorted with derision. "Really, you must stop reading this tripe. It rots the brain."

"*Au contraire*, reading lights up those thinky cells in the old antebellum."

"I suppose you mean cerebellum. These are gossip and celebrity magazines. They are not food for thought. They are empty calories. They decay the teeth."

I suppressed a snigger. "Then *you* should avoid them at all costs."

She glared at me suspiciously. "Why me in particular. What's so funny?"

I managed a look of angelic innocence. Still, it was rather good. She threw down the magazine as Bentley glided in with the coffee.

"Shall I serve the fruity slices now, Sir?"

"What do you say, Alice? Ready to tie on the feedbag?"

"What expressions you use. All right. Thank you, Bentley."

We seated ourselves and did the napkin thingy and sipped our coffee. I was pleased to note that Bentley no longer smelled like stale cooking grease. I inspected Alice carefully for any signs of matrimonial possessiveness and casually threw out a conversational feeler.

"I say, that was... quite an evening last night."

She nodded with satisfaction. "One might say... momentous."

This was not encouraging. "Would one? Wherefore?"

She smiled at me benevolently. "Our minds have never meshed so completely. I believe we came to an understanding."

Panic rose up within me. "My lawyers assure me that I am legally incapable of understanding anything!"

"Don't joke. I want to talk to you seriously, Cyril... about the future."

I hopped from my chair. "What ho! A little early in the day, isn't it?"

"Do stop jumping up and down."

"Well, when you spring things on one like a jack-in-the-box..."

I managed to regain my seat. Alice began again. "Now listen to me... leave the glucose cubes alone, for heaven's sake!"

I abandoned my whimsical take on the Great Wall of China.

"I love you, Cyril, and I know that under that ridiculous affectation you love me too."

"Well, 'love' is a word freighted with nuance."

"Please don't speak. After we're married..."

"Ho!" An uncontrollable spasm caused me to knock my coffee cup clean across the room and send it smashing into a vase that had been in the family for five generations. Truthfully, I had always hated it, but still.

Bentley was crossing the room with a whisk and dustpan before the echoes of the crash had died.

"What's the matter with you, Cyril?"

"I know I was drunk last night, but surely I'd remember if I'd proposed."

"Words are unnecessary when two people love as we do."

"Still, words are wonderful things. Legal things."

"Don't whine. It's unbecoming. It is high on my list of your flaws."

I stared at her. "You keep a list?"

She picked up her handbag with a self-satisfied air and removed a much-creased piece of paper. "I have been curating it since we were fifteen."

"That's rather hard cheese."

"Your use of obscure phrases like that is currently in sixth position."

"May I see it?"

"You may not." She stowed the list back in her bag.

"But seriously, any talk of marriage..."

At this moment Binky made his entrance. He had clearly put a great deal of thought into it. His shoulder entered first, and after a moment of suspense, the back of his head put in an appearance. He waved into the wings as if to an unseen presence.

"Ta-ta my darling. I shall count the hours until I'm with you once again."

He sighed a deep, shuddering sigh and backed fully into the room. Only then did he slowly rotate, revealing a look of mingled bliss and longing. He started upon seeing us. His eyes grew round and his lips pouted like a codfish. He articulated juicily. "So sorry. I didn't suspect this salon was in use."

Alice gave him a look that would delaminate plywood. "Well, it is. And please don't spit in my coffee. We're having a private conversation."

Binky yawned theatrically, stretched and stared off into the distance. "Death before dishonour."

"Death before dishonour."

"Death before dishonour."

Alice glared at Binky suspiciously. "What are you doing in Cyril's house anyway?"

"Just saying goodbye to someone. You don't know her."

Her eyebrows crept into her bouffant and settled in for a protracted stay. "Does she live here? Cyril, who is this woman living in your house?"

I suddenly found myself the object of intense scrutiny. "Who indeed? Yes, I was going to mention that."

"Go on."

Binky was concentrating fiercely, but I could see that this flaw in his backstory had thrown him for a loop. Bentley shimmered up.

"Are you referring to your cousin from the country, Sir?"

"By Jove, yes! Thank you, Bentley! That's exactly who we were referring to."

Alice looked skeptical. "A country cousin! You're full of surprises. What is her name?"

My mind ran in little circles waving its arms desperately. "Er... yes... it's..."

Binky stared at a potted plant by the window. "Gardenia!"

"An unusual name."

"She is as lovely as a flower We are going to be wed."

Alice peered at Binky suspiciously. "How long have you and this Gardenia person been acquainted?"

"Oh, we've known each other for a good while now."

"That's very interesting since I refused a proposal from you only two days ago."

This brought Binky up short, as you can imagine. "I... uh... should have said that we've known each other as friends for some time. Our relationship only flowered into love quite recently."

Alice frowned. "Clearly you have reacted to my refusal by fixating on the first lumpish female that you laid eyes on. You must call this wedding off immediately."

"I will not! This has nothing to do with you. We are soulmates."

Alice threw the full force of her glare at him but Binky barely staggered. She sighed deeply and shook her head. "This is unacceptable. You may take me to lunch tomorrow and I shall untangle this knot for you. I suspect something Oedipal. Now if you don't mind..."

Binky slid up to the dining table like an eight-ball finding the pocket. "I'm famished."

Alice regarded him with astonishment. "I beg your pardon!"

"Oh, sorry," I stammered. "I forgot that I invited Binky to breakfast as well."

"But the table is set for two."

Bentley set down a third plate and began arranging silverware.

"You're hopelessly unromantic, Cyril."

"You can add it to the list."

"It is already at number two."

"What's number one?"

"Your greatest flaw is your lack of any trace of seriousness."

"I see that as a virtue."

"So do many of our generation. I believe it is the great scourge of the age."

Binky was busily stuffing fruity slices down his gullet.

"What is there to be serious about?"

"Don't slurp your food like an animal."

I nodded thoughtfully. "Binky makes a point. Factory-made food has eliminated hunger. The processing of seawater into hydrogen has provided unlimited power. What is there to be serious about?"

"There is more to life than mere subsistence."

I flapped a flipper in a general way. "Look around, old girl. This is a bally sight more than subsistence."

"You live in a prison of privilege. For the masses, life lacks these gewgaws and distractions. Nutrition bars and water in a shack hardly constitute a life well lived."

"I sympathize of course."

"Do not be so quick to congratulate yourself. Our class suffers a different but equally horrible fate. We are being coddled into extinction. We fill the empty hours with shallow entertainments and elaborate social rituals. For example: 'Death before dishonour'..."

Binky looked up from his fruity slices. "Death before dishonour."

"Death before dishonour," I echoed.

"See? We repeat it constantly without any notion of why we do so. What does it mean? Why do we all say it?"

Binky screwed up his face with the effort of thinking. "Well, it's because... death, don't you know... is what comes before... dishonour."

I couldn't let it pass. "I think that's wrong, old bean. I think the idea is that dishonour should come after death. Then it doesn't matter so much... because you're dead, you see."

Alice smirked triumphantly. "You've proven my point. It's an empty ritual that exists to give us the illusion that there is a moral code that gives meaning to life."

"But there *is* a moral code that gives meaning to life. Isn't there?"

Binky had finished his slices and was eyeing mine. "Is there?"

"And what is that code?" inquired Alice.

I gave the old gray matter a good pummeling. "Well... death before dishonour, of course... and don't wear stripes with checks, although I'm toying with the idea of smashing that one to smithereens."

I heard a tiny sigh from Bentley's direction. "I would advise against it, Sir."

Binky jumped in. "A gentleman doesn't perform manual labor."

"Always buy more than you need. That is the mark of the superior man."

"Saving shows a lack of breeding."

"Be true to your club. To insult a man's club is to insult the man."

Alice shook her head grimly. "Don't you see that these ridiculous affectations are not a moral code?"

"Then what's your idea?"

She leaned forward and fixed us with an intense gaze. "Every individual should have the right of self-determination. All humans are equal."

"Let's not lose our heads!"

"Each generation has an obligation to make the world a better place for future generations."

"How do you propose we do that?"

"We must destroy the patriarchy. Nothing can be achieved while our every whim is satisfied by a monolithic industrial complex. I didn't mean to bring this up until after the wedding..."

"Ho!" The cream pitcher followed the coffee cup across the room, destroying a small china figurine. Bentley retrieved the dustpan.

"I beg your pardon, Sir. I should have removed the other breakables from the room after the earlier incident."

"Don't blame yourself, Bentley. It could have happened to anyone."

"For heaven's sake, Cyril, sit down and stop flinging the china."

Binky leaned in, sinking his tie into his coffee cup in the process. "You're saying that life is too easy."

"Since the discoveries that made our modern way of life possible, our class has devolved into effete ineffectual fops. The two of you prove my point."

"Oh, I say, really!"

"A few more generations like this and we'll be apes again."

I rifled through the old brain cells but came up empty. "Sorry, we'll be what?"

"Apes."

"No, doesn't ring a bell."

"They used to live in jungles."

"In what?"

"Oh, never mind! Damn the Great Extinction!"

"But what is there to do?"

"I am one of a band of like-minded individuals that meet in a clandestine fashion to discuss ways of halting the decline of civilization."

"You don't mean you've joined an anarchist cell?"

"Anarchist is a label we eschew. Our group is called, 'Citizens for a Better Tomorrow.'"

"And how will you achieve your lofty goals?"

"By dismantling the current infrastructure through selfless acts of heroism."

I had lost my way at "infrastructure" and struggled to catch up. "I don't quite grasp the gist."

"We shall kick away the crutches that keep mankind from walking into a new tomorrow."

"If you kick away the crutches, mankind will have to *crawl* into a new tomorrow."

"The crutches are metaphorical!"

"Bentley, can you translate?"

"I believe they mean to blow things up, Sir."

Alice nodded. "Exactly."

"What things?"

Alice waved a hand breezily. "Oh, you know, factory farms and hydrogen plants and so on."

I eyed her suspiciously. "Food production facilities?"

"If necessary."

I pounded the table triumphantly. "Weasel-on-Stoat!" I knew it was you!"

"I can neither confirm nor deny whatever you're inferring."

"What do you hope to achieve by depriving civilization of its sandwiches?"

"Sandwiches are the opiate of the people!"

Binky looked forlorn. "Even ham?"

Alice glared at me with gritted teeth. "We discussed all this last night! You agreed! Our minds were one!"

My heart gave a leap. "*That* was our momentous conversation?"

"What did you think it was?"

"Oh, that! Definitely! Thank God!" I had escaped the matrimonial net and was once again swimming in open waters.

"We must return to a time when life took work. When men glistened with the sweat of honest labor—their gleaming muscles flexing under thin, homespun smocks, their women working beside them with heaving breasts... falling into bed at the end of the day to mate like animals. Not the kind of delicate, polite lovemaking you find nowadays but rough, passionate, desperate sex!"

At the word "sex," Binky leaped to his feet, sending his chair crashing to the floor. "Alice is right! I will join you! I will fight beside you! Take me with you to this new tomorrow!"

The air was suddenly filled with the sharp scent of testosterone. I was about to slink under the table and crawl for the door when Bentley placed a shining white plate in front of me with a satisfying clink.

"Your omelet, Sir."

CHAPTER TWO

A Beastly Day at the Club

With great power comes great responsibility or some such drivel. "Noblesse Oblige," don't you know. Nary a hair of Alice Witherspoon had I seen for lo these many days. One assumed that she and Binky were thick as thieves, plotting to murder the firstborn male sons unto the tenth generation and so on. Bentley had come to the rescue, and I was in his debt. Nevertheless, there are times a fellow must take a stand. I mean, once a chap knuckles under to his valet it's not long before he's a serf in his own home. I stood poised... and gazed coldly at the ensemble laid out on the bed.

"Bentley?"

"Sir?"

"Where is the new waistcoat I ordered from Borgen and Bots?"

His triangular nose rose several degrees and gave a discreet sniff.

"Was that a waistcoat? I took it for a pillow sham. The color was so... unusual."

"The color is perfect. I have it on the best authority that everyone will be wearing lavender by Abdication Sunday."

"I am sorry, Sir."

We looked at each other for a long moment.

"Well? Produce the article in question."

"It is at the cleaners."

I gazed at him through narrowed eyes but his face was as placid as a waste-water containment pond on a windless day.

"I have detected a disturbing tendency in you lately to pass judgment on my apparel, Bentley. Is it my imagination?"

"I could not say. I have no imagination. I merely note that your club has very specific rules about one's color palette and that lavender, or indeed any shade of purple, fails to clear the bar."

"Times are a-changing, Bentley. I am the new wind that... sweeps away something or other. Or the new broom. Something new... and sweepy."

"And presumably lavender? Will you be lunching at the club?"

I could see that any victory at this point would be Pyrrhic and threw in the towel with a sigh.

"I imagine so, unless it's Impossible Mutton. I detest Impossible Mutton."

"If Sir would place his arms in the sleeves..."

Dressing for the Club is like donning medieval armor. The girdle, the underclothes, the stockings, the shirt and pantaloons; then the waistcoat, the jacket and sash... and finally the brooches and the shoes—the horrible shoes— shoes that bore no resemblance to a human foot in any dimension.

"Breathe deeply, Sir. The toes will grow numb in a moment."

"Why—that is what I ask myself? What purpose do these thumbscrews for the feet serve?"

"Fashion follows its own logic. I have heard it speculated that impractical shoes demonstrate superiority. One is too rarefied to walk quickly. One will be waited for."

The ormolu clock on the wall jumped in with a hearty chime.

"Goodness, I'm late. Carry me to the car, there's a good man."

Bentley hoisted me as if I were a kitten and glided to the garage where my chariot awaited. This week it was a literal chariot, drawn by six mechanical horses.

"Won't they goggle at the club when I clatter up in this? Where do I sit?"

"I believe you are meant to stand, Sir."

"In these shoes? Not bloody likely."

"You could sit on the floor of the chariot with your legs folded."

"Not very heroic, what?"

"Perhaps not. I did advise against the chariot, if you recall."

"You forget yourself, Bentley. I am the master of my... something or other."

"Fate, Sir?"

"No, it's something to do with fish, I believe."

He stared upward at the ceiling. "Perhaps I am thinking of another expression."

"Now prop me up and punch in the address of the club, there's a good fellow."

As I clattered up one street and down another, clutching desperately to the sides of my chariot, I strove for a look of benign condescension. The hoi polloi parted in front of me. One particularly threadbare group tried to slow my progress by shouting and waving placards, but mechanical horses are illiterate and they were forced to dive out of the way.

Upon arriving at the club, my chariot was blocked by a jeweled palanquin carried by eight turbaned golems. Perched atop it was C. Langford-Cheeseworth. Cheeseworth was a shiny-headed sort of a fellow who affected a louche pattern of speech. His defects of pronunciation had a whimsical way of appearing and disappearing depending on his mood.

"Don't dawdle, Cheeseworth! Some of us have places to be."

"Give one a moment, won't you Cywil? These beastwy shoes keep catching on one another and twipping one."

"Sorry, old trout. I sympathize. Oh, how I miss the embroidered slippers of last season."

"You mustn't regwet the past. It gives you wrinkles."

I noticed another crowd of discontented-looking townsfolk standing across the boulevard with more placards. I was able to make out one sign which stated, "No bread, no peace."

"What do you suppose that's about?"

"Appawently they are devotees of bwead."

"And they lack that particular comestible?"

"Pwesumably."

"Well, there are any number of other foodstuffs. If there is a shortage of bread, let them eat Impossible Mutton, for example. They can certainly have my share."

"There's no pweasing some people. It's all spite and envy. See you inside, dear boy."

I stepped gingerly from my chariot and teetered to the brass-bound door of "Twits"—the club of the Chippington-Smythes since time immemorial. Its brass and Naugahyde were lovingly patched and polished—nothing had changed since my great-grandfather's time—including Evans, the mechanical doorman. "Good morning, Evans."

"Good morning, Sir."

"Did you notice the new chariot? Rather spiffy, don't you think?"

"Yes, Sir. I thought so last week when Mr. Attenborough had it."

"What... *that* chariot?"

"Yes, Sir."

"Last week?"

"Yes, Sir."

"Damn. Listen, Evans, call the manufacturer and have it picked up. I'll find another way home."

"Of course, Sir."

He stared significantly at the top of my head. "I fear our announcement failed to reach you this morning."

"What announcement is that?"

"Amendment to the dress code, Sir. Hats now required."

I glanced around the entry hall and noted the plethora of fanciful headgear. "Drat! Look here, Evans, I will visit the haberdasher first thing tomorrow morning."

He shook his head sadly. "Sorry, Sir. Club rules."

"Well, this is most upsetting."

"We do have some loaners."

"That's all right then. Trot one out."

Evans reached into the coat check and produced a bonnet that resembled a giant tea cozy. I stared at it in horror.

"Don't you have something a bit more stylish?"

Evans gave a rather condescending smile. "If the loaners were too fashionable, there would be no incentive to purchase a hat of your own, would there, Sir?"

As the bonnet passed my nose en route to the old noggin, a familiar odor made its presence known.

"It smells of urine."

Evans looked more closely at the hat in my hands.

"Ah. I'm afraid the Club cat has taken a fancy to that one, Sir."

"And I have to wear this at all times? No respite?"

"Rules, Sir. Without them, all would be fire and flood. We have a hatter on call. There is an extra charge, but of course such trifling sums are beneath your notice."

I settled the malodorous object on my head and trudged grimly to the dining room. Rodgers, the maître d', had been seating me since I was in knee pants. He and Evans were identical models, but I could always distinguish Rodgers by a tiny repair on his left ear—a souvenir of the riots of Oh-Four when the last breeding pair of beef cattle were stabbed to death by Club members insisting on the tradition of the Sunday Roast.

"Good morning, Sir."

"Rodgers. What's the bill of fare today?"

"Impossible Mutton, Sir."

"Is it? Blast! Any chance of a Welsh rarebit?"

"We have a Guatemalan rarebit, Sir, but I really can't recommend it. If your objection to Impossible Mutton is based on the rumor that it contains human flesh, I can assure you that it was denied most vigorously by the manufacturer."

"No, it's the taste I object to—or rather the aftertaste. There's a tang of petroleum jelly that I know some people love, but I can't seem to scrape it off the old tongue."

"I understand, Sir."

"Tell the waiter with the bread basket to stay within my gravitational orbit. By the by, there's a small mob outside that seems keen on acquiring some bread. Perhaps you could fling some rolls their way?"

"I'm afraid not, Sir. Club policy. Table for one?"

"Wouldn't that be paradise? No, I'm meeting my Uncle Hugo. There he is, the bullet-headed old gent waving from behind that potted palm."

My Uncle Hugo was what is known as a serious man. This meant that he knew his net worth to the penny and disapproved of anyone enjoying anything. He wore a tiny black silk top hat that perched on his shiny dome like a sparrow on a monument. As I approached, he stared at my urine-soaked tea cozy.

"What on earth is on your head?"

"Loaner. Didn't get the message. What's that you're sporting?"

"They call it a fascinator. I'm assured it is quite the thing."

"How does it stay on, glue?"

He shook his head sadly. "My God, you look like a damned organ grinder's monkey."

"I might be insulted if I knew what an organ grinder was... or a monkey."

"Monkeys are... or rather were... damn the Great Extinction..."

"I take it they ground their prey's organs into some sort of paste before consuming them?"

"I will not be baited into attempting to educate you. I am not Sisyphus."

"Even if you were, they have medication for that now."

"Sit down before you fall down. Death before dishonour."

"Death before dishonour."

"What ridiculous shoes!"

"They're the latest thing, Uncle. Everyone is wearing them."

"I suppose if everyone cut off their big toe, you'd do it too."

"The shoes would certainly fit more easily."

"You're late. I've ordered your mutton."

"Have you? How kind."

That rather used up Uncle Hugo's conversation for a spell. We sat awkwardly, stealing furtive looks around the dining room and rolling bread into tiny balls. Rodgers paced about the dining room with his gong.

"The North American Beaver has been declared extinct. Polls indicate that the vast majority of the population was unaware of its existence."

He tapped his gong again.

"In business news, the price of human organ futures rose five percent this morning with kidneys up six percent and livers up three percent. Hospitals are swamped as people rush to sell in a bull market."

I waved him over. "I say, Rodgers, these pronouncements are rather gruesome. Isn't the news of the day usually a little more upbeat?"

He leaned in confidentially. "Sales in the dining room have fallen off, Sir, and research has shown that when customers are fearful and anxious, they spend significantly more."

"Do they? Carry on then."

"Yes, Sir. Allow me to mention that smallpox has reappeared in Asia."

He gave his gong a rap and wandered away.

"The end is nigh. Abandon hope, all ye who enter here."

The waiter brought two steaming platters of mutton-like slices swathed in something glutinous. I sighed inwardly.

"Something wrong with your mutton?"

"What? Sorry, I thought I'd sighed *inwardly*."

I slid my mutton around the plate and hid slices under my Beyond Lettuce squares. My uncle attacked his meal like it owed him money and didn't speak again until he had wiped the plate clean with a slice of bread. He sighed and sat back in his chair. "So. You're wondering why I asked you here today."

"It wasn't for the pleasure of my company?"

"It was not. Next week is your birthday..."

"I don't want a big party..."

"I plan no party of any kind. You are reaching the age stipulated in your trust at which your assets revert to you entirely, without restrictions."

A sudden apprehension gripped me. "But I'll still get my allowance?"

"No. You get everything."

I began to panic. "But not my allowance?"

"Try to focus! There will be no need for an allowance. You will possess the entire contents of the trust."

"And what is that?"

"Great thundering cats! Do you have no inkling of what is in your trust?"

"Should I?"

"Yes! You dundering idiot! You will be one of the richest men on the planet! You have a responsibility!"

"To do what?"

"To preserve it. To invest it wisely. To pass it on to the next generation."

"Not really sure I want a next generation. Lot of bother, children and so on."

"There's plenty of time for that. Right now I need you to grasp the seriousness of the situation."

"Who's been running things up until now?"

"The lawyers and financial managers of the trust."

"Can't they keep doing what they've been doing?"

"Well... yes, I suppose so."

"Problem solved. What's for pudding?"

Rodgers came by with his gong. "Lapels will be narrower by three centimeters beginning Wednesday.

Appointments with club tailors can be booked at the concierge desk."

I jumped as a voice suddenly spoke from behind my left ear.

"Do I have the pleasure of addressing Mr. Chippington-Smythe?"

I turned to find a smooth, shiny, round little fellow holding a cylindrical box.

"You do. I'm glad you find it pleasurable. Some of my relations tell me it can be a trial."

He chuckled but I could see his heart wasn't in it. "I am Ahmed Ben Fitzwilliam—the club hatter."

"Ah! Just in the nick of time."

He sadly shook his head. "Indeed, Sir. The hats distributed as placeholders are painful to contemplate."

"And they smell of piss."

"I think we can do better, can't we? Now, what sort of thing did you have in mind?"

"I don't know. Some sort of fedora?"

He recoiled slightly. "Oh, no Sir. That would be most unsuitable."

"Why's that?"

"It's commonplace. We wouldn't want to be commonplace, would we?"

"Heavens no."

"What you want is something original. Something that will excite envy in all who behold you."

I sat up a little straighter in my chair. "And you can deliver such a headpiece?"

"That is my art, Sir."

"I never thought of hat-making as an art before."

"One of the oldest. After all, what is a hat?"

My mind raced. "It's... Hmmm."

He looked at me oddly. "The question was rhetorical, Sir."

"I would have gotten it in a moment, though."

"A hat is a crown that is within the means of the poorest among us. Yes, it keeps us warm in the winter and shades us from the rays of the Summer sun, but these are secondary. A hat, perched just above the organs of sight, is a statement. It tells the approaching stranger everything he needs to know at a glance. Are you timid? Bold? Sexually confused? It is all there in your hat. My job is to ascertain your essence and to create a hat that will announce you to the world."

He opened the cylindrical box in his arms and removed a large, golden sombrero with bright red ribbons cascading down the back.

"Here is an example of my work. This was a commission from Rory Badminton Jones, the actor."

"It's rather gaudy, isn't it?"

He gave a little sniff. "That is the point, Sir. Anyone can slide into a room with a piece of felt on their head that says, 'Don't look at me. I'm not important.' A hat like this says, 'I don't give a damn what you think. I have the confidence to wear this and if you don't like it, you can lump it.'"

"Rather!"

"And while they are staring at the fantastical creation on your head, they are *not* staring at your close-set eyes, your beak-like nose, your lack of chin. All they see is the hat, and you have merely to bask in its reflected glory."

"I say, I'm in!"

He removed a thick sheaf of papers from the hatbox. "Excellent! Fill out this questionnaire and bring it to the concierge desk. Your hat will be delivered to your home in three days."

"But do I have to wear this hideous tea cozy until then?"

"No, Sir. I will loan you this sombrero for the duration."

"Damned generous of you."

I fitted the golden disk on the old dome. It tended to knock into the flowers in the middle of the table, but if I sat very still the staff could still navigate around me. Fitzwilliam gave a little bow.

"Thank you, Sir. I bid you good day."

And off he trundled. Uncle Hugo's sweating pate had turned a deep maroon. He mopped it with his napkin and waved to the waiter. At this point I noticed a rather furtive Binky, sporting a bright green derby, signaling to me from behind a carving station. He widened his eyes and jerked his chin theatrically toward the lobby, then he put his hands in his pockets and sauntered, whistling, out the dining room door.

"Sorry, Uncle Hugo, I've just seen someone I must have a word with."

He squinted at me suspiciously. "You'll consider what I've said?"

"Deeply, richly."

"I have sent you a comprehensive list of your holdings. Will you read it?"

"Unquestionably."

He regarded me doubtfully. "There are no pictures."

"Oh. Well then, I'll have Bentley read it and give me the gist. Ta-ta. Love to Aunt Hypatia."

"You should call on her. She is incomprehensibly fond of you."

"I shall. Tally ho!"

I entered the lobby to find no sign of Binky.

"Psst! Cyril! Over here."

I spotted him then, cowering behind an overstuffed chair.

"Who are you hiding from?"

"No one. I'm not hiding."

"You're crouching behind a chair."

"I... I'm exercising."

"Jolly good. Continue."

He jogged in place for a moment, swinging his arms in random directions and panting. "Death before dishonour."

"Ditto."

He finally ran out of steam and stood catching his breath. "That's better. My blood is positively racing!"

Evans, the doorman, floated up. "Did the gentlemen wish an appointment with the tailors?"

No thank you, Evans. Bentley will see to it."

"Very good, Sir."

Binky looked dejected. "Three centimeters! Shocking. I just had all my lapels let *out*. It's exhausting."

"But one must keep up."

"Why? These constant and capricious changes of fashion are nothing but a means of control! We must throw off the shackles of these tyrannical couturiers!" He suddenly became self-conscious. "Or so I've heard."

"This doesn't sound like you."

"Alice has been teaching me things. She's a pip of a girl, you know."

"Ah, so things are going well with the two of you? I couldn't be happier."

He looked a bit crestfallen. "I suppose it's going well. Mostly she talks and I listen. I've tried any number of stratagems to get her alone in the moonlight but when I do she just natters on about the patriarchy. A fellow doesn't know where he stands."

"Don't give up, old blancmange."

"Oh no, I'll stick to her like a remora, but a fellow likes some encouragement now and then."

We watched the crowd drift past for a tick.

"Is there a reason you summoned me from the dining room?"

"Oh yes, there was something..."

At that moment, Cheeseworth staggered up. He wore a huge creation that depicted a naval battle between competing armadas. Whales spouted and mermaids peeped from the sea foam. He winced with every step he took.

"Ow! If only these shoes weren't so bloody pointy!"

"We must simply bear it until the new fashions are announced. I'm praying for sandals."

"Or espadrilles." His eyes took on a dreamy look.

"That's quite a bonnet, Cheeseworth!"

"Yes, the cannons actually fire, but then the whole hat tends to smolder."

I turned back to Binky. "So, old clot, you wanted to speak to me?"

He glanced at Cheeseworth and his eyes took on a shifty look. "No. Why would I?"

"You gave me a rather significant look and gestured to the lobby with what passes for your chin."

"Did I?"

"You did."

"Oh... um... I wasn't gesturing. There was a bee."

"A what?"

"One of those mechanical bees. It was trying to pollinate me."

"A sterile occupation."

Cheeseworth leaned in conspiratorially. "Don't let me inhibit your conversation. I'm as silent as the gwave."

Binky folded his arms. "I have nothing more to say."

I gazed at him, perplexed. "What an enigma you are today, Binky. How've you been, Cheeseworth?"

"Oh, tolerable. One thought the cwub might cheer one up, but one might as well be in a wax museum. No one in this beastly place ever has the good taste to die. Care for a wubber of bwidge?"

"Sorry, old boy. I must be off."

"Binky?"

"Bridge is the opiate of the people."

"One begs one's pardon?"

"It deadens empathy and distracts from the dissolution of the human race as a species."

"I don't think you're playing it wight."

"I cannot play games of any kind until all are free. It's frivolous."

"Man does not live by bwead alone, dear boy. Without fwivolity, wife is a barren wasteland."

"Nevertheless."

Cheeseworth gave a heavy sigh. "Very well. Perhaps I'll take in the cockfights. Or a bear baiting."

"Are you passing my way?" I asked. "I could use a ride."

"What happened to your chariot?"

"It was obsolete."

Cheeseworth gave a great, honking laugh. "So am I, dear boy. So am I. Come along."

Binky thawed like a frozen fish stick on a windowsill. "I say, room for one more?"

"The more the merrier. Avanti!"

We strolled out front to watch Cheeseworth's palanquin stomp up. The mechanical bearers had a kind of bored look as if to say, "What this? Heavy? Don't make us laugh." We clambered aboard and off they jogged.

"Nifty palanquin, Cheeseworth."

"Do you like it? I'm twading it in tomorrow for a camel caravan encwusted with wubies."

Binky sneered theatrically. "These ostentatious vehicles are the opiate of the people."

"I thought bwidge was the opiate of the people."

"That too. There's opium everywhere if you know where to look."

"Perhaps you should see someone about your obsession with dwugs."

I was having some difficulty keeping my sombrero from blowing off of my head.

"Do you suppose we could unhat ourselves until we reach our destination?"

"Of course, dear boy. This is a very informal palanquin."

"I say, Binky, are you sure there wasn't something you wanted to ask me?"

"Who, me?"

"Yes. At the club, you said there was something...?"

He glanced suspiciously at Cheeseworth and finally shrugged. "Oh well... I wondered if you were going to the country this weekend and whether I might tag along."

"Absolutely. Always welcome."

"And Alice."

"What ho! That's a bit thick."

Cheeseworth cackled. "Alice Witherspoon! The Ivory Empwess! The Toothy Tywant!"

Binky raised an eyebrow. "You are speaking of the woman I love."

"Pardon me, I'm sure."

I sighed with exasperation. "Look here, old Spartan, even you must admit she's a bit of a blister."

"She's changed, Cyril."

"Been to the dentist, you mean?"

"She and I are one now. The struggle has united us."

"Look, Binky, I think it's a simply beastly idea to bring Alice, but if it's what you wish I can deny you nothing. Just don't blame me if the sight of me causes her to flare her nostrils and stamp the earth."

"I'm not afraid."

Cheeseworth drew a jeweled monocle from his vest pocket and screwed it into an eye.

"*I'm* going to the countwy this weekend. Cheeseworth House is minutes away from your chateau. I'll pop over and watch the fireworks. I shall bring my ward, Pansy. You've never met her, Cyril."

"I don't believe so."

"She's absolutely hopeless, but one has a wesponsibility."

"Sounds delightful."

The palanquin bearers stamped to a halt.

"Here we are. Sowwy to hurry you along but those bears won't bait themselves."

I regarded him curiously. "Do you bait them personally?"

"Certainly. I am wuthless. I attack their execrable fashion sense, their lack of wit, their excess of body hair. I make those bears weep, I can tell you."

"Well, good luck. Thanks awfully for the lift, Cheeseworth."

"Think nothing of it. Don't forget your chapeaus. Ta-ta!"

And away he lurched, holding on for dear life. Binky made no attempt to depart, but stood looking at me rather anxiously. I donned my sombrero.

"Spot of tea?"

"No thanks. Got to run. So, we're on for the weekend?"

"Absolutely. Counting on it."

Binky averted his eyes and began kicking at the gravel. "Er... the house is... near Little Climping?"

"You know it is. You've been there dozens of times."

He screwed up his face to indicate heavy thinking and locked his fingers behind his back. "Right, right. It's near that hydrogen plant, isn't it?"

"As you well know. You can see it from the dining room window."

"Good-oh. 'Til the weekend."

He sauntered off in a somewhat serpentine manner, eventually reversing direction and hurrying down the street as if pursued.

I thought it was high time to prove my independence to Bentley and after some experimentation I was able to open the front door by myself. As I stepped into the foyer. I heard a sudden commotion and saw, out of the corner of my eye, an unfamiliar houndstooth-check skirt whipping around a corner. Bentley shimmered into view.

"I say, Bentley, who's that?"

"No one, Sir. Welcome home. May I compliment you on your opening of the front door?"

I eyed him suspiciously but Bentley could give the Sphinx lessons in inscrutability. "I saw someone, didn't I?"

"I think not, Sir."

"Were you in the midst of a romantic liaison, Bentley?"

"Alas, I lack the essential equipment. May I take your sombrero?"

"Thank you. I say, did you get the message from the club about the new dress code this morning?"

"I did, but you had already departed. I regret the incident extremely."

"Things were rather awkward at first, but I am nothing if not resourceful. Put this questionnaire somewhere prominent. I have to fill it out to get my new topper from the club hatter."

"Of course, Sir. Did I see Mr. Wickford-Davies departing in a rather eccentric manner?"

"You did. Binky will be joining us in the country for the weekend."

"Very good, Sir."

"And Alice."

He paused and said gravely, "I see, Sir."

"I'm not happy about it either. You must be extra vigilant."

"My surveillance is ongoing. How is Mr. Wickford-Davies's pursuit of Miss Witherspoon progressing?"

"They are as two cherries on a single stem. I must say, you're a wizard in the Cupid department."

"One does what one can."

"What's in the larder? I'm starved."

"Would Sir care for some pizza rolls?"

"Rather! I'll just peel off these shoes and cauterize my feet."

"Your uncle has sent a rather large package."

"That's a list of my worldly goods. Digest it for me and bring me the... no, that's not a good metaphor. Sift it and bring me the lumps. Well, you know what I mean."

"Of course, Sir."

Perhaps it was something about the light—the late afternoon gloom and whatnot, but a shadow passed suddenly before my eyes and I felt a yawning chasm open in my vitals. "Oh, Bentley... it all seems so meaningless. I really feel I can't go another step."

He looked at me closely. "Did Sir neglect to take his anti-depressant this morning?"

"I don't remember."

"Oopsie Daisy, then."

Bentley lifted me gently and deposited me in my favorite armchair before a roaring hydrogen fire. He tipped two tablets into my palm from a vial he took from his vest pocket.

"Take your nice pills and I'll be back with the pizza rolls in a trice."

I took a sip of water and tossed the pills down the old gullet.

Bentley nodded approvingly. "There might even be a bit of real chocolate after the pizza rolls."

I felt a warm glow begin in my toes and work its way upward. "Real chocolate! Where on earth did you find it?"

"I have my ways, Sir."

I sighed and snuggled back into the upholstery. "I'm all right now. Thank you, Bentley. I don't know how I'd get on without you."

"One feels quite undeserving of such accolades. Shall I bring a ramekin of marinara for dipping?"

"By all means! Let's have a goddam Bacchanalia!"

As Bentley glided off to the kitchen, I wiggled my toes and gazed into the fire. I felt that all was right with the world—an impression that would prove to be sadly misguided.

Chapter Three

A Hot Time at the Old Chateau

Chippington-Smythe House is widely considered to be one of the ghastlier country homes. Nestled amidst mosquito-infested swamps, its crumbling turrets are dwarfed by the massive dome of the world's largest hydrogen plant a mere stone's throw away. Family lore would have it that the house was once a palace fit for an Emperor, but as the family tree dwindled to a few stunted shrubs and country estates fell out of fashion it was allowed to slowly sink into the primordial ooze. I maintained a wing of it for form's sake—run by the formidable Mrs. Oakes—a close cousin of Bentley's from the same factory. Indeed, only a pageboy wig and a spot of rouge kept them from being identical twins.

"Morning, Sir. Coffee-flavoured beverage?"

"Yes. Bless you, Mrs. Oakes."

"There's Cheesy Eggs, Kippered Strips, Morning Links and Improbable Bacon in the chafing dishes. Here's your toast and Fruity Paste. Would you care for anything else?"

"No, that will suffice. Um... real eggs?"

"Almost, Sir."

"Oh well." I scraped some Fruity Paste onto a cold piece of toast. "Have Alice and Binky arrived?"

"Yes, Sir. They've had their breakfast already. They're strolling about the swamp."

"They know to keep to the wooden path?"

"I reminded them, Sir."

"Don't want any guests sinking in the quicksand. Once was quite enough. Thank you, Mrs. Oakes."

"Enjoy your breakfast, Sir."

As she strode away, she passed Bentley, who carried a stack of correspondence.

"Morning, Mr. Bentley."

"Good morning, Mrs. Oakes. Good morning, Sir."

"Bentley! Beautiful day, what?"

"The humidity is unusually low. You have received multiple communications this morning."

"Convey them post-haste. Good news, I hope."

"One slavers with anticipation." He gazed sadly at my wrist. "I pause only to observe that your cuff is currently residing in the Fruity Paste."

"Damn!"

I dabbed at my shirtsleeve with a napkin to no visible effect. Bentley opened the first note.

"Your aunt and uncle will arrive at eleven o'clock."

"Aunt Hypatia and Uncle Hugo?"

"Yes, Sir."

"Why are they coming?"

"The missive does not state their purpose."

"Oh well. The more the merrier I suppose, although Uncle Hugo is a dreadful stick. What else?"

He opened another note. "Mr. Langford-Cheeseworth will arrive at eleven-thirty with his ward."

"Cheeseworth is always good for a laugh. I don't hold out much hope for the ward."

My efforts to remove the paste from my shirtsleeve grew more vigorous. The table began to shake. There was a loud "clink" from somewhere down below.

"May I pour you more coffee beverage, Sir? The previous cup seems to have migrated to the carpet."

"So it has. Clumsy. Pour away. Any more messages?"

"Yes, Sir. You have received a letter announcing, 'New Mumbai chicken-like korma: now with eight percent less acetone.'"

"Well, we must give it a try, mustn't we?"

"If you wish it, Sir."

"They went to the trouble to inform us. It would be ungrateful not to." I munched on my toast. "What kind of Fruity Paste do you suppose this is?"

"The label describes it as 'red,' Sir."

"Not quite so sour as the blue one, is it?"

"I wouldn't know, Sir. I have no sense of taste."

I sipped my coffee beverage and watched the dust motes dance in the sunbeams. "Ah, the country... so peaceful."

The French doors slammed open and Alice strode in, her boots clomping on the parquet floor. Binky trailed behind, gazing at her worshipfully.

"There you are! Do you always sleep the morning away like this?"

"Good morning, Alice. Morning, Binky. Yes, always."

"We shall have to do something about that. Time is too precious to waste. You're not getting any younger, you know."

"So you keep reminding me. Death before dishonour."

"I'm not doing that anymore," she snapped.

"No? The conversation seems naked without it. Binky? Death before dishonour?"

"Sorry, Cyril, Alice won't let me. Thanks awfully for letting us crash."

"Always welcome, dear boy. Open invitation. Carte blanche."

Binky had wandered over to the sideboard and was peering at the contents of the chafing dishes. "I say, are those Kippered Strips?"

He picked up a plate and was about to plow in when Alice raised a dainty fist. "Put that down, Cheswick. You have already had your breakfast."

"But there were no Kippered Strips."

"You are digging your grave with your teeth. You already possess a substantial paunch."

He sagged and put down the plate. "Oh, I say..."

"Cyril, we will be meeting a few friends later. I hope you don't mind. We shall confine ourselves to the gazebo."

"Do I know them?"

"I'm sure not. They do not orbit in our sphere."

"Have at it. Mi casa, etcetera."

There was a bit of a hubbub from down the hall. Above it all I could hear Aunt Hypatia's clarion call.

"There's Aunt Hypatia and Uncle Hugo."

Alice looked sour. "What are they doing here?"

"One hasn't a clue."

"I can't bear that man. Cheswick, come!"

Binky jumped as if he'd sat on a pin. "Yes, dear."

"And don't call me 'dear.'"

"No... Ma'am."

"Oh, you really are hopeless."

They slipped out the French doors to the garden as my aunt and uncle sailed into the dining room. Bentley had to foot it pretty nimbly to nose in before them.

"Mr. and Mrs. Dankworth."

My Aunt Hypatia is a bit of a dragon, but she long ago took me under her scaly wing. It requires some dexterity to avoid her fiery breath but on the whole she's a benign sort of lizard.

"Cyril! Darling boy! Death before dishonour."

"Death before dishonour, Aunt Hypatia. Come to my arms, you glorious creature."

Uncle Hugo stood moodily and estimated the value of the silverware. "Nephew. Death before dishonour."

"Death before dishonour, Uncle Hugo. I hope I see you well."

"Tolerable. Swamp's getting worse."

"Is it? I'll hire some pumps. Have you had your breakfast?"

"Hours ago. Almost lunchtime, isn't it?"

Aunt Hypatia eyed me critically. "You're so thin. You're not eating enough. Bentley, see that he eats."

"Of course, Madame."

I regarded my aunt suspiciously. "To what do I owe the pleasure?"

"I wanted to see my favorite nephew and your uncle wanted to make sure you were doing your homework."

Uncle Hugo glared at me. "Have you read what I sent you?"

"Bentley? Have we?"

"I have sifted it, Sir."

"There, you see? We have sifted it."

"And what are your thoughts?"

"Well, the sifting is only the preliminary exercise. The analyzing is still to come."

"Do not shunt this off. The consequences are substantial."

"Never. Do have some coffee."

My uncle's eyes lit up for a moment. "Is it real coffee?"

"Almost."

He sniffed disdainfully.

"No thank you."

From the drive there came a cacophony that could have been a herd of countertenors being run over by a motorized tank.

"Mr. Langford-Cheeseworth and Ms. Freehold are arriving, Sir."

Through the window I spied a magnificent mechanical procession. "I see they delivered his camel caravan. Rather gaudy. You know Cheeseworth, don't you, Uncle Hugo? From the club?"

"That ridiculous popinjay?"

"That's the one. Show them in, Bentley."

My uncle took on a hunted look. "We can't stay long."

My aunt smacked him on the arm. It would have lamed a lesser man. "Don't be a poop, Hugo. I want to visit with my nephew."

"Very well. I shall be in the orangery."

He hurried off mumbling something about the Circles of Hell. My aunt regarded me shrewdly. "I have something to say to you, Cyril."

Well, this froze my blood, as you can imagine. Aunt Hypatia has strong feelings about how I'm meant to be living my life, and to my certain knowledge there is not one single thing that I am doing correctly.

"Hugo tells me that you expressed doubts about having a family."

"The thought of a brood of screaming children running into the swamp and whatnot rather chills the blood."

"That is unacceptable. This is not a matter of personal preference. You must reproduce. You are the last of the Chippington-Smythes. We cannot be allowed to become extinct."

"It seems rather hard on me."

"You know I love you."

I examined the statement from every angle but I couldn't find the hook.

"I will concede the point."

"You must grow up, Cyril. You must take your place as the head of this family."

"There's plenty of time for all that."

"There is not. It may take years for you to impregnate a wife. The Chippington-Smythes are noted for the immobility of their sperm."

I set down my toast. "This is hardly breakfast talk."

"Heed my words. Find a wife. Have babies. Our family's future depends on you."

I heard approaching footsteps. I could see Bentley pacing down the hallway with Cheeseworth dancing impatiently behind him. Bringing up the rear was, if it was not a trick of the light, the loveliest young lady I had ever laid eyes on. She paced demurely—her eyes cast down in front of her. I heard a buzzing in my ears as if a hive of mechanical bees had nested there. Bentley gave a tip of the head.

"Mr. Langford-Cheeseworth and Ms. Freehold, Sir."

"Cywil! And can this be Aunt Hypatia? You're looking simply marvelous!"

My aunt regarded Cheeseworth with a surprisingly benevolent eye. Apparently, her censure was reserved for blood relations.

"Ah, Mr. Langford-Cheeseworth. How are your parents?"

"Thwiving! Simply thwiving. May I pwesent my ward, Ms. Pansy Freehold."

"Pleased to meet you, my dear. Goodness, you *are* pretty."

The vision spoke in a thrillingly mellow voice. "Thank you."

With that she fell silent and stared at the floor. Cheeseworth seemed accustomed to these lapses in her conversational flow. "Death before dishonour!"

"Death before dishonour."

"Death before dishonour."

Pansy's reply was barely a whisper. "Death before dishonour."

I pawed the ground a bit and began spraying the old Chippington-Smythe charm about pretty liberally. "Pansy, is it? Lovely name."

A fetching blush suffused her cheeks. "It's a flower."

"By Jove, so it is!"

All this wit was apparently too dizzying for Aunt Hypatia. "Well, I'll leave you young people to your fun."

"You're staying for lunch, Aunt?"

"Certainly, if you wish it. I shall join your uncle in the orangery. Until lunch, then."

She sailed down the hall like a clipper ship bound for the Indies. Cheeseworth gazed after her.

"What a magnificent old warhorse she is. I admire her enormously."

"She is the best of aunts. Have you had breakfast?"

"Yes, but one can always find woom for a snack." He lifted the lid of the first chafing dish. "Ooh! Impwobable bacon!"

I waggled my eyebrows winningly at the ward. "What about you, Ms. Freehold?"

"Nothing, thank you."

"Coffee-flavoured beverage?"

"No, thank you."

I searched wildly for something to break the ice. "That's a lovely frock."

This seemed to puzzle her. "Is it?"

"Yes."

"Thank you."

With that we froze into a sort of tableau. I stared at Pansy, she stared at her feet, and Cheeseworth stared at the chafing dishes. Finally, he broke the silence.

"Do you know my favowite thing about the countwy?"

"No, what?"

"Boots! One can wear boots! My feet feel so fwee!"

He lifted the next lid. "I say, cheesy eggs. Good show!"

He resumed grazing. I abandoned all reserve and leapt into the conversational maelstrom. "You live at Cheeseworth Manor I apprehend, Ms. Freehold?"

"Yes."

"How is it we've never met? You're only a few miles away."

"I don't go out much."

"Why would you deprive local society of your company?"

"I don't really fit in."

"I can't believe that."

Cheeseworth cackled into his cheesy eggs. "Believe it, my boy. She's like a deer in the headlights. Has no conversation. Fweezes at the first bon mot."

"Oh, you don't have to worry about that with me. I'm not at all witty."

Cheeseworth gave me a searching look. "I'm glad to hear you admit it. I wasn't sure if you knew it or not."

"Tell me, Ms. Freehold, would you like a tour of the grounds?"

"You don't have to be formal with her, Cyril. He can call you Pansy, can't he my dear?"

She looked away demurely. "If you like."

"Pansy, then. Come, let me show you around the old ancestral manse."

There is a small patch of land behind the estate which looks almost as nature might have intended. Of course, one must ignore the powerful stench of mildew. I breathed deeply, coughed as a cloud of methane drifted past me, and admired the lake at the foot of the hill. Lake Sputum is so pristine one could almost swim in it without antibiotics. In the distance, at the far end of the lake, one could make out the tiny town of Catarrh, with its quaint organ farms and fat rendering plant. There was a twittering from the trees. Pansy lit up with pleasure.

"Oh! Birds!"

"Bird songs, rather. Pipe them through speakers. Used to have animatronic birds but they kept malfunctioning. Falling out of the trees onto one's head. Disconcerting, what?"

She looked down and began digging at the earth with the toe of one shoe. I was growing desperate.

"Like birds, do you?"

"I saw one once in a zoo. It was the most beautiful thing I've ever seen."

The gallant thing to say would have been, "And you're the most beautiful bally thing I've ever seen," but my tongue cleaved to the roof of my mouth and I could only kick at small stones and hum.

"What's that you're humming?"

"What? Oh. I don't know."

"It sounds like the jingle for that breakfast cereal—Frosted Cellu-lo's."

"Does it? I've always been musical. I once thought of being a famous opera singer but there were so many notes and you have to do them in the right order apparently... and of course one would have to learn to sing and so on."

We strolled along in silence for a while. Conversation usually flows from me like water from a breached levee but my usual lines of chatter seemed hopelessly inadequate. Pansy suddenly stopped dead.

"I'm sorry."

"What on earth for?"

"I know I'm a dreadful mope. I have no conversation."

"Not at all. I'm sure you have a deucedly rich inner life. You just want someone to tap the keg and out it will flow."

"No. People always think I'm deep because I'm so quiet, but the truth is I can't stand the sorts of things people talk about. It all seems so... meaningless. It's like we're in a play and everyone knows their lines but me. They do and say improbable things for no discernible reason. I just want a simple life—long walks, a good book by the fire...."

As I gazed into the cerulean disks that poets would refer to as her "eyes," I made a sudden resolution. Pansy would be my bride. We would repopulate the earth with our offspring and all would be joy.

"Are you all right?"

I came back to reality to find Pansy looking at me oddly. "Sorry, what?"

"You were staring."

"Was I? Dreadfully rude. I say, Pansy, I know we've only just met..."

"Pardon me, Sir."

I nearly jumped out of my flannels. Bentley had an unfortunate habit of materializing without warning. I've heard of yoga practitioners that can dis-incorporate their atoms and reassemble them across the room, but Bentley left them in the dust.

"Yes? What is it?"

"You have received a note. 'Our previous announcement, "New Mumbai chicken-like korma: now with eight percent less acetone." should have read, "now with eight percent *more* acetone." We apologize for any misunderstanding.'"

As we rounded the corner of the house, I could see the gazebo through the trees. Alice stood before a somewhat ragged and threadbare crowd, gesticulating enthusiastically. Pansy stared at her.

"Who is that striking woman?"

"The one with the teeth? That's Alice Witherspoon."

"She seems to be quite an orator."

"Oh, Alice could talk the bark off a Spruce tree. I'll introduce you at lunch."

Bentley cleared his throat. "Is there any reply, Sir?"

"To what?"

"To the korma manufacturer, Sir."

"No. You may go."

Down at the gazebo, Binky stood adjacent to the conclave looking miserable. Upon spotting us, he whispered urgently to Alice, who glared in our direction. She made shooing motions to the crowd which rapidly dispersed. Alice strode off toward the swamp and Binky trotted over to join us. I cursed him silently.

Binky eyed Pansy with interest. "Hallo, who's this?"

"Pansy, I'd like you to meet my old friend Cheswick Wickford-Davies—commonly known as Binky. This is Cheeseworth's ward, Ms. Freehold."

He made a rakish little bow. "Charmed, I'm sure."

"Hello."

Binky gave me a significant look. "Look here, old boy, I must speak to you. It's frightfully important."

Pansy turned and started toward the house. "I shall join my guardian in the breakfast room."

Suddenly Binky gave a little hop and snapped his fingers. "No, don't go. Actually... seeing you gives me an inspiration."

I glared at him suspiciously. "Let's not involve Ms. Freehold in one of your schemes. She has only just met you and hasn't built up a protective flight response—like the dodos who had no fear of man and hence were rendered extinct."

Pansy gave a charming little frown. "I am quite capable of judging for myself. Please do not coddle me."

My face grew hot with shame. "I was presumptuous. Please forgive me, dear Ms. Freehold."

"Only if you will forgive me for flying into such a rage. It was quite shameless of me."

"Not at all. I'm an absolute hound. You were right to slap me on the snout." I turned back to Binky, who had fallen into a reverie. "Now, what's stewing in that fevered brain of yours, old squash?"

"It's Alice. She's suspicious."

"That is her defining characteristic."

"When we came to the country, she expected to meet your cousin, Gardenia."

"I have no such cousin."

"Exactly! She believes I am engaged to a woman who does not exist. Bentley's plan has worked perfectly up until now. She's dripping with jealousy and champing at the bit to sink her fangs into Cousin Gardenia and there is no corpus. I am teetering on the brink."

"I don't really see how I can help you."

"It occurs to me..." Here Binky eyed Pansy in a most disturbing way. "...That this young lady may prove the answer to my prayers, if she's game."

Pansy blushed prettily. "I don't know what you mean by 'game' but I'm happy to help you if I can. I believe that we must try at all times to help others. It is a moral imperative."

"By Jove, you're a rum one! Shake on it."

Binky shoved out a paw, which Pansy shook vigorously. Lucky paw!

"Now, here's the plan. You will play the role of my fiancée, Gardenia. During lunch we shall have a tremendous fight and I shall spurn you to the dust. Alice will hurl herself onto my heaving breast and we shall live happily ever after."

Pansy frowned. "This seems an improbable plan. It strains credulity."

"People are used to that where I'm concerned. No one expects me to adhere to logic or consistency."

"But how am I to act in a manner so contrary to my nature?"

"Just pretend you're in a play. Don't you know people who put on a persona very different from their true nature?"

"I have long felt that everyone does it but me."

"There you are, then."

Pansy looked thoughtful. "Perhaps this is an opportunity for me to learn how to fit in."

I fluttered my lashes coquettishly. "Dear Pansy, you don't have to change a jot or a tittle."

"No, I must make an effort. I'll do it!"

"Brave Pansy!"

"Only you mustn't blame me if I'm not very good."

Binky clapped his hands with delight. "You shall be brilliant. I know it."

A shiver ran up my spine. "Perhaps we should run this by Bentley. He's the closest thing to Machiavelli currently in residence."

"Not necessary. It's a perfect plan."

"Don't say that. It makes the hairs on the back of my neck stand up."

Binky was concentrating furiously. "We'll have to let Cheeseworth in on the ruse or he'll blow it all to Kingdom Come."

"I shall speak to my guardian."

"Dear Ms. Freehold, I'm uncommonly grateful."

"Not at all."

Binky stared into her eyes as if he was Svengali and she an aspiring soprano.

"Now remember, I shall be cruel to you, but you mustn't take it personally."

"I never take cruelty personally. That would be selfish."

"Would it?"

"When someone is cruel, they are really expressing their own personal pain. It would be egotistical to make it about me."

"I never thought about it that way. I say!"

Out of the corner of my eye I saw Bentley exit the house carrying a large crate. One of the seedy-looking women from the gazebo appeared in a rather furtive manner and took the crate from him. She wore a houndstooth-check skirt that looked strangely familiar. She scurried off into the bushes and Bentley returned to the house. "Hmm. I wonder what that was all about?"

"What *what* was all about?" Binky inquired.

"Nothing. I must have a talk with Bentley before lunch."

Binky jumped as a distant cannon boomed. "There's the warning cannon. I must change."

"I as well. Pansy, let me escort you back to the house. We shall rendezvous at lunch."

Binky raised a finger. "Now remember, your name is Gardenia, you are Cyril's cousin from the country and we are engaged."

"I believe I apprehend the situation."

"With any luck, Alice will be mine by teatime."

But it would prove to be bitter tea indeed, served with scones of shame and finger sandwiches of pain. And watercress.

CHAPTER FOUR

Luncheon of the Damned

One of the great benefits of country life is the simplicity of the apparel. Girdle, of course—one has standards. But no sash, no brooches and no horrible shoes. As Bentley glided about me adjusting straps and cinching belts, I gazed at him through narrowed eyes.

"I say, Bentley, who was that lady at the back door?"

"Lady, Sir?"

"The one you handed the crate to."

"I really couldn't say, Sir."

"Seedy-looking matron. Houndstooth kilt. She scuttled off into the bushes."

"That seems most irregular, Sir."

"Look here, are you looting the wine cellar? Disposing of the family jewels?"

"To what end, Sir? Money is of no use to me."

"Perhaps she's blackmailing you."

"That would be impossible. My programming forbids me to act against the interests of my employer."

"That's what I always thought."

Bentley got out the old whisk broom and began pummeling me with it as though lint was his hereditary enemy. "Ms. Freehold is quite attractive, Sir."

"Don't change the subject. Do you really think so?"

"My observation is merely academic, of course."

"I intend to marry her, Bentley. I intend to make her 'Mrs. Chippington-Smythe'."

Bentley stopped whisking for a moment. "There are many quotations concerning the course of true love not running smoothly that I could refer you to."

"Pish tosh! Ours is a love without blemish."

"Then I wish you joy, Sir."

He began to whisk me with increased vigor. It was deucedly distracting. "What were we talking about?"

"When, Sir?"

"A moment ago. We were speaking of something."

"I really couldn't say."

The final cannon for lunch boomed forth.

"Luncheon, Sir."

As I stepped into the hallway, I encountered Cheeseworth, who was sporting a jeweled monocle and a gilded walking stick.

"Cywil! What sport! We're to have an impwovisation, are we?"

"Yes, look here, Cheeseworth, don't give the game away, there's a good fellow. Just play along."

"Of course! I shall pway my part with brio! I love an intwigue. It weminds me of my days working as an intelligence agent in the Balkans."

"Really? That sounds dangerous."

"Not weally. In those days we were quite open about it. The embassies would send lists of their spies to each other. It was so much more civilized that way."

"But how did you gather intelligence when they all knew who you were?"

"Alcohol, dear boy. In my experience, anything that cannot be discovered over a whiskey and soda isn't worth knowing."

As we entered the dining room, I found Uncle Hugo and Aunt Hypatia admiring a portrait of one of my distant ancestors. "Cyril, Darling! We're just admiring Great-Great-Grandfather Percy—founder of the family fortune. Such a prominent frontal lobe. Head simply stuffed with brains. Hello, Cheeseworth."

"Dear Hypatia. Death before dishonour."

"Death before dishonour."

"Death before dishonour."

"Death before dishonour. Listen Aunt, before everyone gets here, there's going to be a little..."

As ill luck would have it, Alice strode into the room before I could communicate the meat of the situation.

"A little what, dear?" my aunt inquired.

"Never mind." I leaned in closely. "Just don't be surprised by anything."

"A woman of breeding is never surprised. It shows a lack of foresight."

Alice marched over. "Afternoon Hypatia. How are you, Hugo?"

"Death before dishonour."

"I don't use that phrase anymore."

My uncle stared at her, nonplussed. "What do you mean?"

"I find it hollow."

He opened and closed his mouth a few times and gave the old eyebrows a good shaking. "Do you mean to say that you would not die rather than be dishonoured? Does that concept hold no meaning for you?"

"Not particularly."

"Does tradition mean nothing? The sacrifices of your forbears?"

"Oh... fine! I don't want to get into a philosophical melee before lunch. Death before dishonour, since you insist."

He grumbled into his cravat, "I don't know what the world is coming to."

My aunt gave him a look that could have peeled an orange. "Take a pill, Hugo. Death before dishonour."

"Death before dishonour," quoth I.

"Death before dishonour," echoed Cheeseworth.

Binky rushed in through the French doors.

"Am I late? Death before dishonour."

He froze, staring at Alice like a mouse spotting a cobra. "Oh! Sorry, dear!"

The steam was fairly rising off of her. "It's fine."

Cheeseworth began the roundelay. "Death before dishonour."

"Death before dishonour."

"Death before dishonour."

"Death before dishonour."

Alice fumed for a moment and then spat through the jagged stumps that lurked behind her pale lips. "Death before dishonour."

Pansy floated into the room. She wore something diaphanous and blue. My heart did a quick turn around the block, then stood in place hopping up and down like a pogo stick. She kept her eyes demurely low.

"Good afternoon. Death before dishonour."

We all glanced sideways at Alice.

"Oh God!" She gritted her teeth, which took some doing as the upper and lower jaws had few points on which they agreed. "Death before dishonour."

"Death before dishonour."

"Death before dishonour."

"Death before dishonour."

"Death before dishonour."

"Death before dishonour."

Aunt Hypatia examined Pansy. "What a lovely dress."

"Is it?"

"It is."

"Thank you."

Binky pulled out a chair and gave Pansy a look. "Sit here by me... Gardenia."

My aunt wrinkled her forehead which caused a small avalanche of powder to burst loose and cascade down her cheeks. "Gardenia? I thought her name was Pansy."

"Yes. Pansy is short for Gardenia."

"No, it's not."

"Well, they're both flowers."

"I suppose that's true."

Bentley glided over. "Excuse me, Sir."

"Yes, Bentley?"

"A message has arrived. It states that users of Chumley's tooth polish are twice as likely to marry the mate of their choice."

I eyed Pansy hungrily. "Thank you, Bentley. Order me five or six dozen."

"Of course, Sir."

Cheeseworth took a seat and patted the chair next to him. "Sit between Binky and I, Gardenia."

Alice glared at Pansy poisonously. "So! This is the country cousin I've heard so much about."

Binky gave a choked little cough. "Gardenia, allow me to introduce you to Alice Witherspoon."

"Yes, I saw you orating earlier. You are a powerful speaker."

This threw Alice off her stride. "Well... thank you."

"I envy you enormously. I can't speak in front of people. Too shy."

"Nonsense. It only takes practice."

"No. Some people are just braver than others."

"How is it we've never met, Ms... is it Ms. Chippington-Smythe?"

"No, Freehold."

"And how are you and Cyril related?"

Uncle Hugo sat up. "What?"

My aunt shoved the bread basket at him. "Take a roll, Hugo." She leaned forward. "Go on, my dear."

Time to stick my oar in. "Yes. Well... you know... there was that branch of the family from..."

"Dusseldorf, wasn't it?" asked Cheeseworth quickly.

I seized the proffered rope. "Yes! Dusseldorf! The Dusseldorf Chippington-Smythes."

Uncle Hugo was growing red. "What?"

"Don't interrupt, Hugo."

"Oh, I say..."

My aunt had a hungry gleam in her eye. "So, you were brought up in Dusseldorf, my dear?"

"Yes, until I was twelve."

"And you speak German?"

I winked at her madly with the offstage eye. "Well, of course they didn't speak it at home. I mean, it's such a deucedly guttural form of communication."

The hint was lost on Aunt Hypatia. "But you spoke German when you went out, amongst the Germans?"

"Oh yes."

"How lovely. Say something."

"I beg your pardon?"

"Now, Aunt, she's not a performing dog, you know!"

"I love the sound of German. I studied it as a child. *Wo hast du in Dusseldorf gelebt?*"

Binky turned positively green. He stared at Pansy like a castaway hoping for a sail on the horizon. Time seemed to elongate. Pansy was as placid as a woodland pool.

"*Wir hatten ein kleines Haus am Friedrichstradt. In der Nähe des Krankenhauses.*"

I stared at her with new found admiration. "I say!"

Aunt Hypatia regarded her shrewdly. "Fascinating."

All this had gone rather over Alice's head. "And what brought you here to Chippington-Smythe House?"

Cheeseworth stared up at the ceiling thoughtfully. "Well, her family was killed in a twagic boating accident..."

"And she had nowhere else to go," I added.

"A chilling tale!"

I gave her a hard stare. "Yes, Aunt, but of course all this is ancient history to you."

The penny dropped at last. "Oh, indeed!"

"Look here," Uncle Hugo sputtered.

"Hugo! The crudités!"

"But... Oh, blast!"

Alice turned back to Pansy. "And when did you and Cheswick meet?"

"We met here, in the country. He had come up for the Fall foliage..."

Binky leaned in. "Yes, but there was acid rain the entire weekend and we were trapped in the house."

"So, I suggested we play hide and seek..."

"And she hid so well I didn't find her until the day I was to leave..."

"By then I was starving of course, and dehydrated."

"I nursed her back to health... spooned broth into her and rubbed lotion onto her chapped feet..."

"He was an angel."

"I proposed before she recovered from her delirium."

"When he told me later that I had accepted I was overjoyed."

Cheeseworth clapped his hands. "What a whirlwind womance! Like something fwom a fairy tale!"

Alice picked sourly at a roll. "It sounds rather hasty to me."

"That's what makes it so wonderful! We hardly know each other. There is so much still to discover."

Binky gave Pansy a dazzling smile. "Please pass the crudites, my love."

She looked back at him gravely. "But my darling... you are allergic to crudités."

"Am I?"

"Yes. Deathly allergic."

He suddenly comprehended the plot. "But, see here, that's my funeral! If I choose to endanger my health, what business is it of yours?"

"Your welfare and mine are intertwined. You are no longer eating crudités for yourself alone. You are masticating for two now."

"This is intolerable! I will not be dictated to!"

He seized an item from the crudité platter and bit down with a loud crunch.

"Reckless man! Put down that cellulose stick at once!"

My uncle pounded the table. "By God, you stand your ground, Sir."

My aunt turned to him. "Yes, Hugo? You have something to say?"

He deflated like a cold souffle. "That is... nothing."

"I thought not."

Pansy rose to her feet. "How can you speak to me so?"

"A man has certain prerogatives."

"I am your fiancée!"

"If our opposing views on crudités are indicative, this will be a marriage rife with controversy."

"Are you saying...?"

"Yes! I release you from your promise!"

Alice seized a cellulose stick and bit it in two. "Good show, Cheswick! Finally, some backbone!"

"Oh... how could you?"

"You must remember that I am a man."

Cheeseworth leaned in. "If you're not going to eat the cwudités could you slide them over here? I'm simpwy ravening."

Binky slammed his hands down on the table. "Damn the crudités, say I!"

Alice stared at Binky. "Cheswick! I have never seen this side of you! I must say..."

"Yes! This is the real me! A man of action. A man of principle."

Bentley sidled up and murmured in my ear. "Shall I serve the soup, Sir?" he murmured.

"Not now, Bentley. We're approaching catharsis."

"Very good, Sir."

Binky had the bit between his teeth. "I am a man who takes what he wants."

"Yes!" Alice moaned softly.

"Alice!"

"Yes, Cheswick?"

"Will you..."

"Yes? Yes?"

Suddenly Pansy made a dramatic gesture. "Wait!"

"What?"

"Wait!"

"Why?"

"I do not wish to be set free!"

Cheeseworth threw down his roll. "Twist!"

I could see Binky going through the script in his head trying to figure out where he had gone wrong. "But..."

"Passion such as ours must necessarily combust from time to time, but there is too much between us to simply walk away. "

Binky licked his lips nervously. "Look here, what are you...?"

"She's saying, 'Don't throw the baby out with the bath water,' what?" Hugo grunted.

Binky's eyebrows danced a tarantella. "Gardenia, may I speak to you privately?"

"Anything you have to say you can say in front of my family."

"But they're not... oh, damn it!"

Alice glared at Pansy. "Cheswick, will you allow yourself to be dictated to?"

"No, I bally well will not!"

Pansy stepped close to Binky and laid a finger across his lips. "Listen to me, my love." She gazed deeply into his eyes. Fortunate eyes! She took a deep breath, inflating the chiffon cloud that enveloped her. Binky goggled.

"No one on earth could possibly love you as I do. I wish to bear your children. I wish to grow old with you. I know with every fiber of my being that I can make you happy. Stay with me, my love."

And then she kissed him. And when I say kissed, it was rather as if she sucked his soul out from between his teeth. I could almost hear his resistance pop like a soap bubble. Cheeseworth tore at his bread nervously.

"Gardenia, aren't you wather... forgetting yourself? One is twying to eat, after all."

When they parted I could see that Binky was a dead duck.

"Cheswick! What is the meaning of this?"

Binky looked around dreamily. His eyes tried to focus on Alice. "What? Oh, hello Alice. I didn't hear you come in."

"Am I to understand that you still intend to marry this woman?"

Binky emerged from his trance. "Yes, by God, I do!"

He and Pansy locked lips again and I abandoned myself to despair. The castles I had built on air came crashing down. I motioned to Bentley.

"Bentley, you may serve the soup."

CHAPTER FIVE

Showdown at the Hydrogen Plant

Love is rather like a diving bell. Those inside it are deaf to the outside world. They breathe each other's air and hear only the echoes of each other's voices. The crushing pressures of the world around them touch them not at all. Those outside the bubble, however, are highly susceptible to the buffeting currents and predatory fish that surround them. While Binky and Pansy floated dreamily in each other's eyes I struggled to survive the maelstrom that had erupted in the dining room.

Alice stamped a tiny hoof. "Cheswick! I will not be ignored!"

Cheeseworth, who was rapidly emptying the crudité platter, lifted an eyebrow. "I say, Binky, this does wather cwoss the line, what?"

Uncle Hugo simply looked bewildered. "Will someone explain to me what the bloody hell is going on?"

"Sit still, Hugo. When there is something that requires a response from you, I will inform you."

"Here now, let's all calm down, shall we?" I protested weakly.

Alice slapped a palm on the Chippendale. "I will not calm down! I know when I am being trifled with. Cheswick!"

Binky shook himself like a dog awakening from a dream of bones. "Hmm? Yes?"

"You and I have embarked upon a great enterprise. Will you abandon it for the sake of this... person?"

"Sorry, what?"

"We have sworn oaths. The moment approaches. Will you stand with me?"

Binky suddenly snapped back to reality. "Oh! Sorry, Alice. I'm afraid I'll have to bow out." He gave Pansy a shy glance. "Things have changed, rather."

Alice threw down her napkin. "I have not changed! Very well, I shall carry on alone, if need be. I discard you on the ash heap of history."

"Thanks awfully, old girl. I knew you'd understand."

Alice carefully placed her chair under the table and faced me. "Cyril, I must depart."

"But they're just bringing the soup."

"The soup is immaterial! Matters of great pith and moment are afoot. Farewell!"

And with that, she pounded across the parquet and whooshed out of the French doors. There was a moment of stunned silence before Cheeseworth turned back to his plate.

"Good widdance, say I. How can one enjoy one's food with those gweat ivory plaques clacking against each other like mah-jongg tiles?"

Bentley entered, pushing the serving trolley, its wheels squeaking cheerfully. "The soup, Sir."

"Ah! What are we having, Bentley?"

"Clam-like chowder, Sir."

"Rustic, what?"

Binky and Pansy had locked lips again and sounded like a defective squeegee on a dirty window. Cheeseworth watched them sourly. "Look here, now that she's gone, you two can snap out of it. She is my ward, after all."

Aunt Hypatia gave a satisfied grunt. "Ah! The light begins to dawn."

"Not to me," grunted my uncle.

"Of course not, Hugo. Eat your soup. This little play was for Alice's benefit."

I dipped into the chowder, which was larded with tiny gray nuggets of something that tasted like carpet lint. "Yes. It was intended to arouse her jealousy, but it seems to have gone rather off the tracks. Look here, you two, come up for air, will you?"

I threw a half-eaten roll at Binky's head but, due to my deficient throwing skills, it caught Pansy on the ear. She started and looked around in surprise.

"Where has Miss Witherspoon gone?"

"Stalked out like a panther."

"But we weren't done!"

"Afraid the curtain's come down. La Comedia e finita and all that."

"Oh no! I've spoiled everything!"

Binky put a hand around her waist. "Not for me, my darling."

Pansy removed his hand with a grimace. "You don't need to call me darling now that she's gone."

"But... we're in love!"

"Don't be silly! That was only acting!"

A sudden surge of hope made me rise from my seat. "Hello!"

"Bwavo! Didn't know you had it in you, my dear."

"Acting?" stuttered Binky.

I jiggled up and down on the balls of my trotters. "She was acting! She doesn't love him at all!" I grinned at my aunt. "Did you hear, Aunt? It was just for show!"

My aunt squinted at me as if attempting to gauge the level of my mental disorder. "You enthusiasm is excessive, Nephew. Perhaps Bentley should provide you with a sedative."

Pansy wrung her hands. "I was building to a climax! I was going to have second thoughts in a moment and cast you aside. Oh... I told you I wouldn't get it right."

Binky began to melt. His chin sank into his chest, which was already sliding toward his abdomen. "Are you saying... you don't care for me?"

"Goodness no. I don't even know you."

"But then... Oh, dash it all! Now what do I do?"

I beamed at Pansy. "I say, that was rather spiffy with the German. How did you do it?"

"I speak five languages."

Cheeseworth shook his head gloomily. "I told you she doesn't fit in. Spends all her time studying. Physics, Fwench, Organic Chemistry. I don't know what I'm going to do with her."

Binky dropped into his chair looking as though life had given him a stiff kick in the shins. I admit to a certain amount of satisfaction which I tried to disguise behind a sympathetic expression.

"I'm afraid you've rather exploded your chances with Alice, old cock."

At the mention of Alice, Binky's eyes started from his head.

"Alice! Where is she?"

"Gone, and left you on the ash heap of history if memory serves."

He stared about wildly. His hair, which normally assumed a laissez faire attitude toward life positively stood on end.

"My God! She's going to do it!"

"Do what?"

"Listen, Cyril, we've got to stop her! Call the police!"

"I'm sure she's not that desperate."

"You don't know her."

"I know her well enough to know she's not about to end it all because of a ruined romance with you."

"You don't understand! She's been plotting it for weeks."

"Plotting what?"

"She and her anarchist friends... they're going to blow up the hydrogen plant!"

The company regarded Binky with varying degrees of concern. Aunt Hypatia was the first to speak.

"What, the hydrogen plant we can see from the window?"

"Yes!"

"But that would blow us up too."

"Hence my sense of urgency."

I am a man of action. I did the sensible thing. "Bentley!"

"Sir?"

"You heard?"

"I have already set things in motion, Sir."

"We've got to stop her!" cried Binky.

Cheeseworth dusted the breadcrumbs from his lap. "My cawavan is at your disposal."

I leaped to my feet. "Quickly, everyone! To the camels!"

If one is trying to move with urgency, mechanical camels are not the optimal form of transport. They lurch and sway to an alarming degree. Aunt Hypatia could ride anything and Bentley was imperturbable, but the rest of us hung on for dear life. Poor Uncle Hugo wound up facing backwards and let out a constant stream of curses. The hydrogen plant slowly drew nearer. I leaned over to Bentley.

"What will we say to them when we get there? They'll never let us in."

"I believe you will find them compliant."

"How can you be so sure?"

Bentley regarded me gravely. "Because you own the hydrogen plant, Sir."

"I what?"

"In sifting through the contents of your trust I discovered that it was your great-great-grandfather, Percy Chippington-Smythe who discovered the secret of converting sea water into hydrogen. You own them all, Sir."

I stared at Bentley. The world seemed to have gone all silent. "All the hydrogen plants?"

"Indeed, Sir. If you will forgive me for saying so, I believe that was part of Miss Witherspoon's attraction to you. She hoped that by marrying you she would gain access to your hydrogen plants for the purpose of blowing them up."

"What ho, a little wounding to the old ego."

"Her desire to destroy your gas facilities was undoubtedly mingled with a deep affection for you, Sir."

"No doubt."

Bentley cleared his throat—a purely theatrical exercise since his throat is simply a flexible metal tube. "I do wish Mr. Wickford-Davies and yourself had consulted me about your stratagem. I would have made some salient points."

"Too late for crying over spoiled milk."

"Spilt, Sir."

"What?"

"Spilt, not spoiled."

"Really? I like mine better."

"No doubt those who catalog folk wisdom will revel at your input. With regard to Miss Witherspoon..."

I held up a hand whose manicure was somewhat the worse for wear. "A moment, Bentley. Uncle Hugo!"

"What?"

"I own the hydrogen plant!"

"I know!"

"I told you I did my homework."

"Blast your homework! How do you steer these bloody camels?"

The air was filled with mechanical brays.

"One didn't have time to wead the instruction manual!" Cheeseworth cried.

I strained to see through the cloud of dust that surrounded us. "I think I see her. She's just going through the gate."

"Where are the guards?"

Binky kicked his camel, which gave a loud "clang" and refused to quicken its pace. "Her gang was to overpower them. They're inside now waiting for her with the explosives."

Bentley drew up next to me. "As I was saying, Sir..."

"In a moment, Bentley. We must formulate a plan."

Pansy timidly raised a hand. "I studied the schematics of these hydrogen facilities when I wanted some light reading. To do any real damage they will have to place the explosives against the containment vessel. Once we enter the main door we turn right. The wall of the containment vessel is roughly one hundred metres from the entrance."

"What an interesting girl you are. Bentley, did you get that?"

"Yes, Sir, but if you would allow me..."

"No time! Follow me!"

I led the caravan past the guards at the gate, who lay hog-tied and gagged. My aunt eyed them doubtfully.

"Shouldn't we untie them?"

Binky was adamant. "There's not a moment to lose! They must be deploying the explosives by now. "

Hurling ourselves from our jeweled dromedaries we raced through the entryway and down the corridor. In the distance we could hear a babble of voices. Alice's voice pierced through them like a trumpet.

"Let the new world begin!"

We sped around the corner to find Alice lighting the end of a long, black fuse. Behind her crowded the motley crew from the gazebo. I spotted Bentley's houndstooth-clad matron among them. The fuse sparked and began to travel toward a large mound of crates.

Binky stood forth. "Stop!"

Alice's eyes rolled wildly in their orbits. "Too late! Run for your lives! This plant will be a crater of cinders in a matter of moments!"

At this point in the proceedings, things became rather chaotic. The ragged band of anarchists scrambled for the exit.   Only Alice and her houndstoothed henchwoman stood in our way. Uncle Hugo stared nervously after the departing revolutionaries.

"I say, Hypatia, perhaps we'd better..."

"Hugo, stay!"

"Yes, dear."

My aunt widened her stance and glared at Alice. "I demand that you put out that fuse at once!"

"Never!"

Binky peeped out from behind Bentley. "I say, Alice, you'll be exploded, you know."

"But so will you!"

"Now look," Binky stammered, "I know I've behaved like a bit of a ass, but that's no reason to blow everyone to pieces."

"This has nothing to do with you!" Alice looked nervously behind her at the shortening fuse. She turned back to us. "If I try to escape, will you promise not to douse the explosives?"

"Of course not!" huffed my aunt.

Alice gave a sigh and planted her feet more firmly. "Then this is it. I suppose it's better to go out in a blaze of glory than to grow old filled with regret at having missed a chance to make the world a better place."

Pansy gazed at Alice wonderingly. "How I admire your idealism! If you were not intent on killing us all I believe we could have been friends."

Cheeseworth barked a bitter laugh. "You're coming out of your shell at last, are you? Shame we'll all be blown to smitheweens in a moment."

Pansy smiled at her guardian. "You're being very brave."

"Oh, I'm tewwified! But wunning is so gauche."

To my mind there seemed to be a distinct lack of fuse dousing going on. "I say, Bentley, lend a hand, will you?"

"Have no fear, Sir. All will be well."

"But the fuse!"

At that moment the fuse disappeared inside the nearest crate. I formed myself into a roundish lump and prepared to meet my maker. Moments passed and we remained demonstrably alive.

Alice goggled. "Why this lack of combustion? This is unacceptable. I demand an explanation."

Her houndstoothed compatriot stood forth. "Alice Witherspoon, I arrest you in the name of the law!"

"What is the meaning of this? Have I harbored a viper in my bosom?"

"I am not a disaffected anarchist as you supposed. Rather I am Police Officer Cleary of The Yard!"

"But it was you who procured the explosives!"

"Thanks to Mr. Bentley I supplied you with false explosives that contain harmless quantities of peat moss and bicarbonate of soda."

I stared at my valet with amazement. "Bentley? Is this true?"

"Allow me to explain. When Sir tasked me with redirecting Miss Witherspoon's affections, I naturally began to gather intelligence to assist in the necessary planning. Upon discovering her involvement with an anarchist movement intent on destroying the underpinnings of society I enlisted the aid of the constabulary who dispatched Officer Cleary to infiltrate their community."

"That's who I saw that day at the house, nipping around the corner."

"Indeed, Sir. It was she who provided Miss Witherspoon with the harmless simulations in these crates."

"By Jove, you're a wonder."

"You exaggerate my abilities as always, Sir."

Aunt Hypatia harrumphed. "But the rest of the saboteurs have escaped."

"No Ma'am," Officer Cleary chuckled. "My officers were waiting at the entrance to apprehend them. It only remains to transport them, along with Miss Witherspoon, to the police station for processing."

Alice had been following all this with her jaw hanging open. This had the unfortunate side effect of making her teeth more visible. Suddenly she saw the trap closing.

"You'll have to catch me first!"

Alice had run the hundred at university and still had a wicked kick. As she was about to round the last of her pursuers, Cheeseworth stuck his jeweled walking stick between her legs and sent her sprawling. It was the work of a moment for Officer Cleary to slap the cuffs on her.

I slapped Cheeseworth on the back. "Well, that's that. I say! Bit of excitement, what?"

"One hasn't perspired *comme ça* in eons."

"What's next, Bentley? Soup still hot, do you think?"

"I believe the police will want a statement from you, Sir. As the owner of the facility, you will be asked to bring charges against the perpetrators."

"Oh bother! I'm famished."

"I placed New-cumber sandwiches in your left jacket pocket, Sir. Wrapped in a napkin. There is a thermos of tea in the right pocket."

I reached into my pocket and wouldn't you know, he'd done it again. It was like a conjurer's trick. "What a treasure you are. Aunt Hypatia? New-cumber sandwich?"

"Thank you, Cyril."

"Uncle Hugo? Cheeseworth? Pansy?"

We munched on finger sandwiches as we were transported to the police station. Upon arriving we found Binky in a rather grim cell surrounded by anarchists.

"Hello, My Lad! Death before dishonour."

At this there was a general uproar, with some crying, "Death before dishonour!" and some loudly proclaiming that the phrase oppressed the people and should be stricken from the language. Binky pressed up to the bars.

"Cyril! Tell them I'm not a saboteur."

"But can I be certain? Which of us can peer into the secret hearts of our fellows, what?"

"Oh, I say."

"Courage, *mon vieux*. I'll have you out of there in a jiffy."

With Bentley's help I sorted through the paperwork and arranged Binky's release. The anarchists, at Bentley's suggestion, were charged with trespassing, which called for a fine but no imprisonment.

"They were led astray, Sir, by Miss Witherspoon's considerable magnetism."

"What are we to do about Alice?"

Aunt Hypatia stepped forth. "You cannot send her to prison."

I gaped at her in astonishment. "But she lit the fuse! She intended to blow us all to kingdom come."

"Nevertheless, she is one of us. Incarceration is out of the question."

"It's simpwy not done, dear boy."

"Drat! But where does this leave me? Is she still determined to graft her life to mine? And what of the beautiful Pansy?"

Binky's nostrils flared. "I saw her first."

"You most definitely did not."

"But I declared my love for her first."

"You love Alice."

"Alice loves you."

Cheeseworth looked around.

"I say, where *is* Pansy?"

Bentley materialized at my elbow.

"At my suggestion, she has gone to the interrogation room to comfort Miss Witherspoon."

Binky stuck out what passed for his chest. "Let's put it to her. Let her choose."

"Fine. Bentley, lead the way."

Binky and I stalked behind Bentley cheek by jowl, glaring at each other. Upon reaching the interrogation room, Bentley threw open the door to reveal Alice and Pansy wrapped in a passionate embrace, their lips melding in a mind-bending kiss.

"It would seem that Ms. Freehold has made her choice, Sir."

The lovers broke apart. Pansy put her fingers to her lips. "Your teeth tickle."

"Oh, I say," Binky softly sighed.

Cheeseworth screwed in his jeweled monocle. "Bwavo, Pansy. The girl has undreamt of depths."

As we walked back to the waiting room, I took a sanguine view.

"Well, at least Alice will leave me in peace now."

"That was my aim, Sir."

Binky glared at Bentley resentfully. "But what of me?"

"Yes, Sir... upon reflection I felt that marriage to Miss Witherspoon was not an optimal outcome for you. I do apologize."

"No, you're right. I know you're right."

"I say, Bentley, is the loving couple in the interrogation room your doing?"

"I believe so. I was present when Ms. Freehold first beheld Miss Witherspoon and the attraction was apparent to me at once. At lunch I observed that Miss Witherspoon was equally drawn to Ms. Freehold. I felt certain that if they were left alone, their mutual affection would manifest itself."

"Gads! I don't know how they stuffed all those brains into that noggin of yours."

"Most gratifying, Sir."

Binky sat heavily on a bench. "What a beastly weekend this has been."

"What you need is something to take your mind off it all. What about joining Cheeseworth at a bear baiting?"

"Wegrettfully, the season has ended."

"Or a cockfight. What about it, Cheeseworth?"

"I'm competing in one this Wednesday! Do come. It's for the League Cup. I've been twaining for weeks."

Binky began to show signs of life. "Well... it does sound like fun."

"It's settled, then. Bentley, pack my things. We're going back to town."

"Very good, Sir."

We fled at breakneck speed back to my urban keep, where I instructed Bentley to pull up the drawbridge, lower the portcullis, release the hounds and kick any interlopers into the moat. Soon there were tantalizing odors from the auto-cooker wafting through the air. Ensconced in my jewel box of a study with my comfy old dressing gown wrapped around me, I stared into the hydrogen fire and pondered recent events.

"It was a close call, wasn't it, Bentley? Without hydrogen the world as we know it would cease to exist."

"I believe that was Miss Witherspoon's intent, Sir."

"But now we can go on as before... visiting the club, weekends in the country, purchasing ever more elaborate toys. Do you know, I sometimes feel it's all a bit pointless."

"Surely not, Sir."

I was struck with a horrifying thought. "I say, Bentley... you don't suppose Alice was right about everything? That having all our wants taken care of turns us into helpless, effete fops? That income inequality hurls millions into lives of despair? Have I been on the wrong side all along?"

Bentley had retrieved the mail from a side table and was leafing through a periodical. "Oh, look Sir, the new issue of 'Gentleman's Apparel' is here. The shoes this season look extremely comfortable!"

"What? Hand that over at once!" I quickly scanned the pages. "Flats! Rounded toe box. Heaven!"

"I shall order a selection at once."

I sighed and settled back in my chair. "Oh, Bentley, what a season it's going to be."

"Indeed, Sir."

"What was I talking about?"

"When, Sir?"

"Just now. I was asking your opinion about something."

"Was it in regard to shoes?"

"No. Something else. Oh well, it can't have been very important."

The distant strains of "Lady of Spain" wafted in from the front door.

"Who on earth could that be?"

"Excuse me, Sir."

Bentley wafted away and I stared into the fire. He returned carrying a large, cylindrical box.

"Am I expecting a delivery?"

"I fancy it's your new hat, Sir, from the Club."

"But I never got a chance to fill out the questionnaire."

"I took the liberty of filling it out for you."

I regarded him gravely. "It was a rather personal survey, Bentley, designed to ferret out my essential nature. The hat within will reveal your true evaluation of my character."

"I hope you will not be disappointed."

I confess my hands trembled a bit as I unwrapped the package. No man is a hero to his valet and Bentley had seen me at my worst. Surely the chapeau within would be a chimera composed of equal parts vanity, vapidity and pettiness. I lifted the lid to find... a beautiful, dove-gray fedora with a plain silk band. The lines were exquisite. I lifted it onto the old noggin and it fit like a dream.

"I don't know what to say."

"No words are needed, Sir. If you are satisfied that is enough."

"No... No, it's not enough. Bentley..."

"Sir?"

"Be so good as to burn that lavender vest."

"Thank you, Sir. I have already done so."

I snuggled into the cushions and pushed my toes closer to the fire. "I'm so happy, Bentley. This really is the best of all possible worlds."

He set a tray with a shining white plate on my lap. "Indeed, Sir. Now eat your nice cheesy omelet while it's hot."

And that is exactly what I did.

The End

If you enjoyed Bentley's chronicle of my first adventure, I implore you to pop over to Amazon and leave a little review.
You can click on this hilariously incomprehensible link:

https://www.amazon.com/dp/B0B1QWQKNL
Your reviews are the inflated bladder which keeps this series afloat.
If you'd like advance notice on the next book's release head to:

WWW.TwitsChronicles.com
where you can sign up for something called an email list and where you can ask me and my friends a question which I or they may answer in the next newsletter.
I hate spam (with the exception of the delicious pork product that has been unfairly tarred by association), so I shall keep emails to a minimum.

Afterword

Cyril, Bentley and The Usual Suspects will return in:

TWITS in Peril

Read on for a taste:

When the world is too much with us; when even the strongest anti-depressants have lost their power to soothe; when the music of life is drowned out by the rough chants of striking postal workers—one can always depend upon one's club. As I waited for my cocktail, I gazed at the brass and Naugahyde, whose patina derived from centuries of careful polishing by the staff—some of whom were as old as the club itself. Sven the bartender, for example, had been lovingly patched and repaired since my great-great-grandfather's day. He could remember when steak and kidney pie contained actual steak and kidneys. It must have been a savage time—members feasting on the organs of slaughtered animals. Now, of course, the animals are gone, along with the fish in the sea and the birds of the air, but Twits, my beloved club, remains.

Sven set a tumbler before me with two fingers of amber perfection sloshing from side to side. I stared at it gloomily. It was perfect yesterday, perfect today... it would be perfect tomorrow. Where was the spice of life to be found?

"Your brandy and Paxil, Sir."

"Thank you, Sven. Has Mr. Wickford-Davies been in today?"

"Not yet, Sir."

I raised the glass and gazed at the play of light shining through it.

There was a sudden flurry and a nasal bray from the doorway. "A moment, if you please, Mr. Chippington-Smythe!"

I turned to see the club's beady-eyed Marshall, Cubby Martinez cruising toward me like a uni-browed shark. If anyone could be described as my nemesis, it was he. I don't know from whence Cubby's animus derived. I suppose there was something in my scent that aggravated a primal instinct within him. He gripped a yardstick in his hairy paws.

"I'll just check those heels if I may."

I extended my feet. "Measure away, Cubby. You won't find any irregularities here. Not with Bentley on the job."

He snapped the yardstick next to my shoes and crouched down to peer at the number.

"Satisfied?"

He frowned at the yardstick. "I suppose it meets the requirements... barely, but if you get any wear on the rubber tips you'll be in violation."

I tossed my drink down the old sluice and waved a flipper at him. "When that day comes, Cubby my lad, there will be fruity pops in Hell."

He sniffed. "Just doing my job."

"Is it my imagination or are your eyes growing closer together? I ask merely for information."

Cubby's retort was lost in the sudden hubbub as a couple of old chums came rolling up to the bar. Ford and Lincoln had been my accomplices in many a schoolboy caper.

"Cyril, old shoe! Death before dishonour."

"Hallo, Ford. Hallo, Lincoln. Death before dishonour."

Ford peered at me with concern. "How goes the struggle?"

"You're looking rather hipped," observed Lincoln.

"Yes, I've got a touch of the Blue Meanies, I'm afraid."

"Here, Sven, a round of Brandy and Prozacs here. You just chug that down. That'll put you right."

Ford turned to Cubby, who was still gripping his yardstick. "Hallo, Cubby."

"Sir."

"Why don't you stick that yardstick somewhere inappropriate?"

Cubby reddened slightly. "Just enforcing the dress code."

"Fending off the barbarous hordes, eh? Carry on."

Lincoln sipped at his B and P and looked at me. "What've you got to be blue about? Riches beyond compare, young, bachelor. You ought to be kicking up your heels. Seems rather ungrateful of you."

"Money isn't everything," I muttered gloomily.

"It's a lot, though."

"I don't know. Sometimes I think the economically disadvantaged are happier than we. Their lives are so simple."

Lincoln screwed up his forehead. "I don't think that's true, old fish."

"It *is* true. They get food, shelter and hydrogen for free. They don't suffer under the cruel lash of fashion. I've seen them wearing shorts and flip-flops. Flip-flops! A far cry from the six-inch heels we're tottering around in this month."

Lincoln admired his calves. "You must admit they make your legs look fabulous!"

I sighed and stared down into my glass. "I dream sometimes of what it must be like to live as they do."

That got a hearty laugh from Ford. "You wouldn't last a day."

"Of course I would! A gentleman can fit in anywhere."

He gave a hoot and kicked back on his stool. "What'll you bet?"

"Seriously?"

Lincoln set down his tumbler. "Say, I'm in. I'll bet you can't live like the huddled masses for... let's say a week. Loser pays the winners' bar tab for a year."

Those who know me will tell you I have a weakness for gambling. My valet, Bentley, has often had to speak to me about it. Bentley, however was at home. It is difficult not to blame him for what followed. He usually has a kind of instinct that warns him when I'm about to get into trouble so that he can swoop in to save the day, but even if he had set out from home at the first mention of the bet, he wouldn't have arrived at the club in time to save me.

About The Author

Born in Canton Ohio and raised in a box made out of ticky-tacky, Tom Alan Robbins spent his youth as a middle-aged character actor. He has appeared in nine Broadway shows, including *The Lion King* in which he created the role of Pumbaa. He recently received a Grammy nomination for the cast album of *Little Shop of Horrors*. He has maintained a parallel career as a writer, penning scripts for TV shows like *Coach* and writing plays, one of which (*Muse*) recently won the New Works of Merit Playwriting Competition.

The Twits Chronicles series is his first attempt at novel writing and it has been a pure joy. He hopes to keep creating adventures for Cyril and Bentley as long as there are readers who enjoy them.

39550364R00065